COLONIAL AND POSTCOLONIAL AFRICA

EDITED BY
ROSINA BECKMAN

Britannica®
Educational Publishing
IN ASSOCIATION WITH

ROSEN
EDUCATIONAL SERVICES

Published in 2017 by Britannica Educational Publishing (a trademark of Encyclopædia Britannica, Inc.) in association with The Rosen Publishing Group, Inc.
29 East 21st Street, New York, NY 10010

Distributed exclusively by Rosen Publishing.
To see additional Britannica Educational Publishing titles, go to rosenpublishing.com.

First Edition

Britannica Educational Publishing
J.E. Luebering: Executive Director, Core Editorial
Anthony L. Green: Editor, Compton's by Britannica

Rosen Publishing
Amelie von Zumbusch: Editor
Nelson Sá: Art Director
Michael Moy: Designer
Cindy Reiman: Photography Manager
Bruce Donnola: Photo Researcher

Library of Congress Cataloging-in-Publication Data

Names: Beckman, Rosina, editor.
Title: Colonial and postcolonial Africa / edited by Rosina Beckman.
Description: First edition. | New York : Britannica Educational Publishing in Association with Rosen Educational Services, 2017. | Series: The colonial and postcolonial experience | Includes bibliographical references and index.
Identifiers: LCCN 2016022148 | ISBN 9781508102793 (library bound)
Subjects: LCSH: Colonies—Africa—History. | Postcolonialism—Africa. | Africa—History—1884–1960. | Africa—History—1960– | Africa—Politics and government.
Classification: LCC DT29 .C572 2016 | DDC 960.3—dc23
LC record available at https://lccn.loc.gov/2016022148

Manufactured in Malaysia

Photo credits: Cover (inset) Print Collector/Hulton Archive/Getty Images; cover (background), p. 24 AFP/Getty Images; p. iii Wolfgang Kaehler/LightRocket/Getty Images; pp. viii-ix Hougaard Malan Photography/Gallo Images/Getty Images; p. ix (inset) British Museum, London, UK/Bridgeman Images; p. 4 Biblioteque Nationale, Paris, France/Archives Charmet/Bridgeman Images; p. 13 Michel Desjardins/Gamma-Rapho/Getty Images; p. 30 Central Press/Pictorial Parade; p. 39 ullstein bild/Getty Images; p. 45 Felix Lipov/Shutterstock.com; pp. 57, 67 Courtesy of the National Portrait Gallery, London; p. 59 Encyclopaedia Britannica/UIG/Bridgeman Images; p. 63 Photo © Tallandier/Bridgeman Images; p. 97 Underwood Archives/UIG/Bridgeman Images; p. 101 Photo © AGIP/Bridgeman Images; p. 116 Binh Thanh Bui/Shutterstock.com; p. 121 Pictures from History/Bridgeman Images; pp. 125, 150, 201, 220 Encyclopædia Britannica, Inc.; p. 129 Photo12/Universal Images Group/Getty Images; p. 143 Universal History Archive/Universal Images Group/Getty Images; p. 158 Science & Society Picture Library/Getty Images; p. 172 John Moss/Black Star; p. 175 Courtesy of the Senat, Paris, photograph, J.E. Bulloz; p. 182 AP; p. 215 Photos.com/Thinkstock; p. 228, Van Hoepen/Hulton Archive/Getty Images; p. 264 Margaret Bourke-White/The LIFE Picture Collection/Getty Images; p. 272 Camera Press/Globe Photos; p. 279 Keystone/Hulton Archive/Getty Images; p. 292 © AP Images; cover and interior pages patterned border element zizar/Shutterstock.com, background and border colors and textures Rawpixel.com/Shutterstock.com, Alted Studio/Shutterstock.com; back cover pattern pzAxe/Shutterstock.com.

CONTENTS

CHAPTER THREE

INTRODUCTION

Between November 15, 1884, and February 26, 1885, the major European nations held a conference in Berlin, Germany, at which they met to decide all questions connected with the Congo River basin in Central Africa. The general act of the Conference of Berlin declared the Congo River basin to be neutral, guaranteed freedom for trade and shipping for all states in the basin, forbade slave trading, and rejected Portugal's claims to the Congo River estuary. Strange as it may seem that a meeting of Europeans in Germany would determine the power structure in Central Africa, the conference was the result of Western colonialism—the exploration, conquering, settlement, and exploitation of large areas of the world by the nations of Europe between the 16th and 20th centuries.

Africa has a long history of entanglement in Western colonialism. The age of modern colonialism began about 1500, following the European discovery of a sea route around Africa's southern coast in 1488. The Europeans hoped that the new sea route would provide them direct access to valuable trade goods, such as silk and spices, from Asia. However, they quickly became interested in Africa as more than just a stop on the way to Asia. Gold came from Central Africa by Saharan caravan from Upper Volta (Burkina Faso) near the

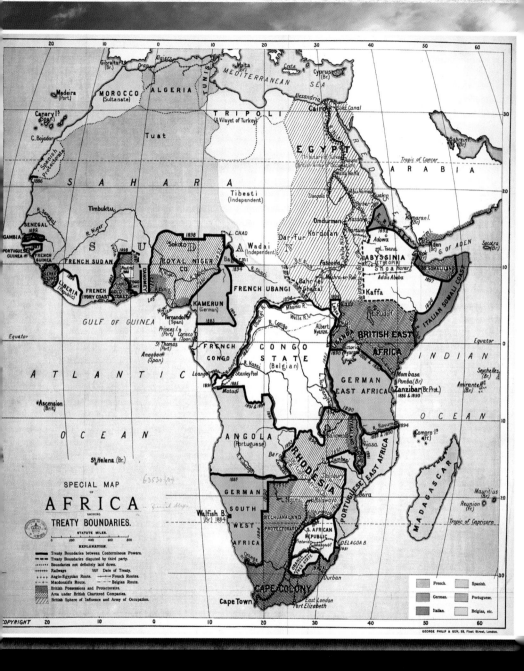

This map of Africa dates from 1891. You can see the borders that the European nations decided on and the lands they each claimed.

Niger, and interested persons in Portugal knew something of this. When Prince Henry the Navigator undertook sponsorship of Portuguese discovery voyages down the west coast of Africa, a principal motive was to find the mouth of a river to be ascended to these mines. The Portuguese thereby became the first colonial power in Africa, though theirs was less a territorial empire than a commercial operation based on possession of fortifications and posts strategically situated for trade. The Dutch, French, and British soon established outposts and forts in West Africa to compete with the Portuguese and eventually forced them out.

Slavery, though practiced in Africa itself and widespread in the ancient Mediterranean world, had nearly died out in medieval Europe. It was revived by the Portuguese in Prince Henry's time, beginning with the enslavement of Berbers in 1442. Portugal populated Cape Verde, Fernando Po (now Bioko), and São Tomé largely with black slaves and took many to the home country, especially to the regions south of the Tagus River. African slaves were imported into Spain's New World possessions in the early 16th century, as well as into the Portuguese possession of Brazil and, somewhat later, into the British colonies of North America. However, it was not until the development of sugar, cotton, and tobacco plantations in the Americas that the Atlantic slave trade reached huge proportions, exceeding any such earlier trade. The British became the major traders in slaves, although the French, the Dutch, and others also took part. African societies that had not participated in the slave trade prior to the European presence began to do so. Small African states that lay near the coast served as suppliers to the Europeans and grew into sizable empires because of their new wealth and power. Ashanti and Oyo in West Africa are examples. They supplied European merchants with slaves that they obtained through warfare with neighboring states.

In 1807 the British government declared the slave trade illegal and ordered British merchants to cease trading in slaves. States that had traded directly with the British were forced to find new ways to support themselves; Ashanti, for example, began to export kola nuts to its northern neighbors. A number of African societies put slaves to work in activities such as mining gold and raising peanuts, coconuts, sesame, and millet for the market. Other Africans continued to trade slaves with Europeans who did not accept Britain's decree. The British navy patrolled the West African coast during the first half of the 19th century to enforce the abolition, but slave dealers moved their operations southward; even some slaves from

East Africa were sent to the Americas. In many areas slavery was not abolished effectively until the Europeans established their colonial presence late in the 19th century. Until then, Europeans could not stop internal African slavery because they did not have any power or influence beyond the coast.

In the mid-19th century, the European colonial presence was confined to Dutch and British settlers in South Africa and to British and French military personnel in North Africa. The discovery of diamonds in South Africa and the opening of the Suez Canal, both in 1869, focused European attention on the continent's economic and strategic importance. A scramble among European powers to claim African territories soon followed.

By the turn of the 20th century, the map of Africa looked like a gigantic jigsaw puzzle, with most of the boundary lines having been drawn in a sort of game of give-and-take played in the foreign offices of the leading European powers. The division of Africa, the last continent to be so carved up, was essentially a product of the new imperialism, vividly highlighting its essential features—a notable speedup in colonial acquisitions and an increase in the number of colonial powers. In this respect, the timing and the pace of the scramble for Africa are especially noteworthy.

Before 1880 colonial possessions in Africa were relatively few and limited to coastal areas, with large sections of the coastline and almost all the interior still independent. By 1900 Africa was almost entirely divided into separate territories that were under the administration of European nations. The only exceptions were Liberia, which was founded in West Africa in the early 19th century as a home for freed American slaves and generally regarded as being under the special protection of the United States; Morocco, conquered by France a few years later; Libya, later taken over by Italy; and the ancient country of Ethiopia, which remained a monarchy until 1974.

The second feature of the new imperialism was also strongly evident. It was in Africa that Germany made its first major bid for membership in the club of colonial powers: between May 1884 and February 1885, Germany announced its claims to territory in South West Africa (now Namibia), Togoland, Cameroon, and part of the East African coast opposite Zanzibar. Two smaller nations, Belgium and Italy, also entered the ranks, and even Portugal and Spain once again became active in bidding for African territory. The increasing number of participants in itself sped up the race for conquest. And with the heightened rivalry came more intense concern for preclusive occupation, increased attention to military arguments for additional buffer zones, and, in a period when free trade was giving way to protective tariffs and discriminatory practices in colonies as well as at home, a growing urgency for protected overseas markets. Not only the wish but also the means were at hand for this carving up of the African pie. Repeating rifles, machine guns, and other advances in weaponry gave the small armies of the conquering nations the effective power to defeat the much larger armies of the peoples of Africa. Rapid railroad construction provided the means for military, political, and economic consolidation of continental interiors. With the new steamships, settlers and materials could be moved to Africa with greater dispatch, and bulk shipments of raw materials and food from Africa, prohibitively costly for some products in the days of the sailing ship, became economically feasible and profitable.

Penetration of Islamic North Africa was complicated, on the one hand, by the struggle among European powers for control of the Mediterranean Sea and, on the other hand, by the suzerainty that the Ottoman Empire exercised to a greater or lesser extent over large sections of the region. Developments in both respects contributed to the wave of partition toward the end of the 19th century. First,

Ottoman power was perceptibly waning: the military balance had tipped decisively in favour of the European nations, and Turkey was becoming increasingly dependent on loans from European centres of capital (in the late 1870s Turkey needed half of its government income just to service its foreign debt). Second, the importance of domination of the Mediterranean increased significantly after the Suez Canal was opened in 1869.

The partition of Africa below the Sahara took place at two levels: (1) on paper—in deals made among colonial powers who were seeking colonies partly for the sake of the colonies themselves and partly as pawns in the power play of European nations struggling for world dominance—and (2) in the field—in battles of conquest against African states and tribes and in military confrontations among the rival powers themselves. This process produced, over and above the ravages of colonialism, a wasp's nest of problems that was to plague African nations long after they achieved independence. Boundary lines between colonies were often drawn arbitrarily, with little or no attention to ethnic unity, regional economic ties, tribal migratory patterns, or even natural boundaries.

In some areas the Europeans used military force to conquer territory. In others, European and African leaders came to an understanding about mutual control over territory. These agreements were essential to the Europeans because they could not have controlled all of their colonial territory otherwise. They needed the consent of those African political leaders who saw an advantage for themselves in associating with the European powers. However, other African people continued to resist European control throughout the colonial period.

Britain, France, Portugal, and Belgium controlled the largest amount of territory in Africa. Germany also had several African territories, though it lost them after its defeat in World War I. Although styles of rule varied from country to country, in general the colonial powers made little effort to develop their colonies, except as sources of raw materials and markets for their manufactured goods. Africans were, by and large, excluded from participation in the decisions that affected their lives. European settlers established themselves in parts of Africa where the land was fertile and the climate relatively temperate, often pushing Africans off the best land with the help of colonial administrators.

Decolonization was one of the most striking developments of the mid-20th century. The colonial empires that once seemed so stable dissolved as the European powers, weakened by World War II, proved unable to resist the rising tide of nationalism. The process has been a lengthy one, however, often marked by bloodshed.

The first in sub-Saharan Africa were Ghana (formerly Gold Coast), from the British, in 1957, and Guinea, from the French, in 1958. Most of the remaining French colonies became independent in 1960 and most of the British colonies shortly thereafter. The transfer of power in most British and French territories was to educated Africans who had served in the colonial government. Usually these Africans had been educated in mission schools and then in European universities.

In general, independence proceeded most easily in countries where Europeans had worked mostly as colonial administrators or businessmen and had not established permanent homes. In countries where large numbers of Europeans had settled and lived for generations, independence proved more painful. The Algerians forced the French to recognize independence in 1962 only after a long and costly war, and the Portuguese colonies in Africa finally gained independence in the mid-1970s after 15 years of guerrilla warfare and a revolution in the home country. In 1965 the white minority in Rhodesia unilaterally declared independence from Britain rather than share power with the Africans. Many years of negotiation and warfare elapsed before they agreed to the establishment of the multiracial country of Zimbabwe in 1980. In late 1988, after 73 years of control over South-West Africa, which was Africa's last colony, South Africa agreed to grant independence. After a transition period, the colony became the independent country of Namibia in 1990.

CHAPTER ONE

NORTHERN AFRICA

• •

A frica north of the Sahara is differentiated from the rest of the continent by its Mediterranean climate and by its long history of political and cultural contacts with peoples outside of Africa. It is physically separated from the rest of the continent by the Atlas Mountains and is inhabited primarily by peoples who speak languages belonging to the Afro-Asiatic group. Those peoples include, for example, the Imazighen (or Berbers; singular Amazigh) of Morocco, Algeria, and Tunisia. The Berbers are most numerous in Morocco and least in Tunisia, where, as a result of culture contact and intermarriage, they have become largely assimilated with Arabs, who speak a Semitic language. The Arabs migrated into North Africa from Arabia in a number of waves; the first of those waves occurred in the 7th century CE. The distinctive nature of Maghrebian, or western Arab, culture resulted from that admixture. While the country of Egypt, which lies to the east of the Maghrib, is on the African continent, it will not be discussed here because it is also considered part of the Middle East and is discussed in the volume of this series entitled *The Colonial and Postcolonial Middle East.*

At the time when Europe began its colonial expansion in the Maghrib—starting with the French occupation of Algiers in 1830—the region was divided into four political entities. Morocco, ruled by the ʿAlawite dynasty, was a sovereign country. Algeria, Tunisia, and Libya were autonomous states that recognized the religious authority of the Ottoman sultan. The French occupation of Algeria had direct and serious con-sequences for the authority of the rulers of Tunisia and Morocco and, indirectly, for the authority of the rulers of Libya as well. A French protectorate was eventually imposed on Tunisia in 1881–83, and in Morocco in 1912. A year before that, Libya was invaded by Italy. World War II brought major changes to North Africa, promoting the cause of national independence. A reaction to years of colonialism had set in and was erupting into strong nationalist tendencies in each of the four countries of the region.

ALGERIA

The customary beginning date for the events immediately leading to the French invasion of Algeria is in April 1827, when Ḥusayn, the last Ottoman provincial ruler, or dey, of Algiers angrily struck the French consul with a fly whisk. This incident was a manifest sign of the dey's anger toward the French consul, a culmination of what had soured Franco-Algerian relations in the preceding years: France's large and unpaid debt. That same year the French minister of war had written that the conquest of Algeria would be an effective and useful means of providing employment for veterans of the Napoleonic wars.

The French conquest of Algeria began three years later. The dey's government proved no match for the French army that landed on July 5, 1830, near Algiers. Ḥusayn accepted the French offer of exile after a brief military encounter. After his departure, and in violation of agreements that had been made, the French seized private and

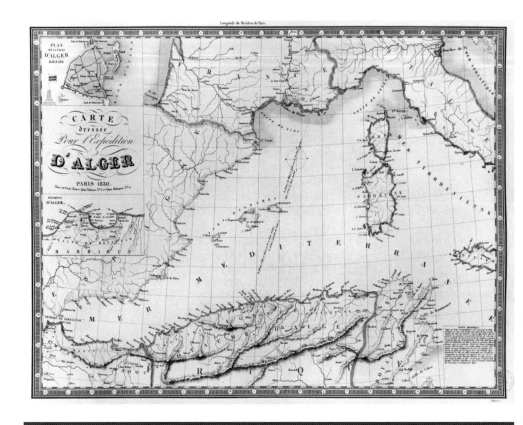

This map from 1830 was drawn up for the French expedition that invaded Algeria that year. It shows Algeria's Mediterranean coast (*bottom*), as well as the coastlines of nearby nations.

religious buildings, looted possessions mainly in and around Algiers, and seized a vast portion of the country's arable land.

The first years of colonial rule were characterized by numerous changes in the French command, and the military campaign began to prove extremely arduous and costly. The towns of the Mitidja Plain—

just outside Algiers—and neighbouring cities fell first to the French. General Camille Trézel captured Bejaïa in the east in 1833 after a naval bombardment. The French took Mers el-Kebir in 1830 and entered Oran in 1831, but they faced stiffer opposition from the Sufi brotherhood leader, Emir Abdelkader ('Abd al-Qādir ibn Muḥyī al-Dīn), in the west. Because towns and cities were plundered and massacres of civilian populations were widespread, the French government sent a royal commission to the colony to examine the situation.

During their campaign against Abdelkader, the French agreed to a truce and signed two agreements with him. The treaty signed between Abdelkader and General Louis-Alexis Desmichels in 1834 included two versions, one of which made major concessions to Abdelkader again without the consent or knowledge of the French government. This miscommunication led to a breach of the agreement when the French moved through territory belonging to the emir. Abdelkader responded with a counterattack in 1839 and drove the French back to Algiers and the coast.

France decided at that point to wage an all-out war. Led by General (later Marshal) Thomas-Robert Bugeaud, the campaign of conquest eventually brought one-third of the total French army strength (more than 100,000 troops) to Algeria. The new military campaign and the initial onslaught caused widespread devastation to the Algerians and to their crops and livestock. Abdelkader's hit-and-run tactics failed, and he was forced to surrender in 1847. He was exiled to France but later was permitted to settle with his family in Damascus, Syria, where he and his followers saved the lives of many Christians during the 1860 massacres. Respected even by his opponents as the founder of the modern Algerian state, Abdelkader became, and has remained, the personification of Algerian national resistance to foreign domination.

Abdelkader's defeat marked the end of what might be called resistance on a national scale, but smaller French operations continued, such as the occupation of the Saharan oases (Zaatcha in 1849, Nara in 1850, and Ouargla in 1852). The eastern Kabylia region was subdued only in 1857, while the final major Kabylia uprising of Muḥammad al-Muqrānī was suppressed in 1871. The Saharan regions of Touat and Gourara, which were at that time Moroccan spheres of influence, were occupied in 1900; the Tindouf area, previously regarded as Moroccan rather than Algerian, became part of Algeria only after the French occupation of the Anti-Atlas in 1934.

COLONIAL RULE

French rule in Algeria was characterized by violence and mutual incomprehension between the rulers and the ruled. There was a relative absence of well-established native mediators between the French rulers and the mass population, while an ever-growing French settler population (the colons, also known as *pieds noirs*) demanded the privileges of a ruling minority in the name of French democracy. A large-scale program of confiscating cultivable land made colonization possible. The colons accounted for roughly one-tenth of the total population from the late 19th century until the end of French rule.

It is difficult to gauge in human terms the losses suffered by Algerians during the early years of the French occupation. Estimates of the number of those dead from disease and starvation and as a direct result of warfare during the early years of colonization vary considerably, but the most reliable ones indicate that the native population of Algeria fell by nearly one-third in the years between the French invasion and the end of fighting in the mid-1870s.

Gradually the European population established nearly total political, economic, and social domination over the country and its native inhabitants. At

THE ROOTS OF ALGERIAN NATIONALISM

Algerian nationalism developed out of the efforts of three different groups. The first consisted of Algerians who had gained access to French education and earned their living in the French sector. Often called assimilationists, they pursued gradualist, reformist tactics, shunned illegal actions, and were prepared to consider permanent union with France if the rights of Frenchmen could be extended to native Algerians. This group, originating from the period before World War I, was loosely organized under the name Young Algerians and included (in the 1920s) Khaled Ben Hachemi ("Emir Khaled"), who was the grandson of Abdelkader, and (in the 1930s) Ferhat Abbas, who later became the first premier of the Provisional Government of the Algerian Republic.

The second group consisted of Muslim reformers who were inspired by the religious Salafī movement, which was founded in the late 19th century in Egypt by Sheikh Muḥammad

'Abduh. The Association of Algerian Muslim 'Ulamā' (Association des Uléma Musulmans Algériens; AUMA) was organized in 1931 under the leadership of Sheikh 'Abd al-Hamid Ben Badis. This group was not a political party, but it fostered a strong sense of Muslim Algerian nationality among the Algerian masses.

The third group was more proletarian and radical. It was organized among Algerian workers in France in the 1920s under the leadership of Ahmed Messali Hadj and later gained wide support in Algeria. Preaching a nationalism without nuance, Messali Hadj was bound to appeal to Algerians, who fully recognized their deprivation. Messali Hadj's strongly nationalistic stance, or even the more muted position of Ben Badis, could have been checked by such gradualist reformers as Ferhat Abbas if only they had been able to show that step-by-step decolonization was possible. Several efforts to liberalize the treatment of native Algerians, promoted by French reformist groups in collaboration with Algerian reformists in the first half of the 20th century, came too late to stem the radical tide.

the same time, new lines of communication, hospitals and medical services, and educational facilities became more widely available to Europeans, though they were dispensed to a limited extent—and in the French language—to Algerians. Settlers owned most Western dwellings, Western-style farms, businesses, and workshops. Only primary education was available to Algerians, and only in towns and cities, and there were limited prospects for higher education. Because employment was concentrated mainly in urban settlements, underemployment and chronic unemployment disproportionately affected Muslims, who lived mostly in rural and semirural areas.

WORLD WAR II AND THE MOVEMENT FOR INDEPENDENCE

World War II brought with it the collapse of France and, in 1942, the Anglo-American occupation of North Africa. The occupation forces were to some extent automatically agents of emancipation; both Allied and Axis radio stations began to broadcast in Arabic, promising a new world for formerly subject peoples. The effect was further heightened by the June 1941 promise of emancipation for both Syria and Lebanon, given by the Free French and backed by the British authorities in the Middle East.

Ferhat Abbas drafted an Algerian Manifesto in December 1942 for presentation to Allied as well as French authorities; it sought recognition of political autonomy for Algeria. General Charles de Gaulle declared a year later that France was under an obligation to the Muslims of North Africa because of the loyalty they had shown. French citizenship was extended to certain categories of Muslims three months later, but this did not go far enough to satisfy Algerian opinion. A display of Algerian nationalist flags at Sétif in May 1945 prompted French authorities to fire on demonstrators. An unorganized uprising ensued, in which 84 European settlers were massacred. The violence and suppression that followed resulted in the death of about 8,000 Muslims (according to French sources) or as many as 45,000 (according to Algerian sources). The main outcome of the massacres, however, went far beyond the human losses. They became the foundation for the Algerian War of Independence, which began nearly a decade later. The demonstrations were the last peaceful attempts by Algerians to seek their independence.

The French National Assembly voted for a statute on Algeria on September 20, 1947, in which the country was defined as "a group of departments endowed with a civic personality, financial autonomy, and a special organization." The statute created an Algerian assembly with two separate colleges of 60 members each, one representing some 1.5 million Europeans and the other Algeria's 9 million Muslims. After lengthy debates the statute was passed by a small majority. Muslims were finally considered full French citizens with the right to keep their personal Qur'ānic status and were granted the right to work in France without further formalities. Military territories in the south would be abolished, and Arabic would become the language of educational instruction at all levels.

The law was poorly implemented, however, and the subsequent elections were widely held to have been manipulated to favour the French. Most of the reforms laid down by the statute were never enforced. In spite of this, Algeria remained quiet. The principal change had been the fact that some 350,000 Algerian workers—five times as many as in the post–World War I period—were able to establish themselves in France and remit money to Algeria.

THE ALGERIAN WAR OF INDEPENDENCE

Nationalist parties became increasingly radical as they realized that their goals were not going to be achieved through peaceful means. The war began on the night of October 31, 1954. The movement, led by the FLN

(Front de Libération Nationale, or "National Liberation Front"), issued a leaflet stating that its aim was a
sovereign Algerian state. It advocated social democracy within an Islamic framework and equal citizenship

In this photo from 1955, French soldiers in Algeria's Aurès Mountains
are checking the identity papers of native Algerians as part of their
campaign against Algerian resistance to French rule.

for any resident in Algeria. Two weapons would be used: guerrilla warfare at home and diplomatic activity abroad, particularly at the United Nations (UN).

The armed uprising soon intensified and spread, gradually affecting larger parts of the country, and some regions became guerrilla strongholds beyond French control. France became more involved in the conflict, drafting some two million conscripts over the course of the war. A French army of 500,000 troops was sent to Algeria to counter the rebel strongholds, while the rebels collected money for their cause and took reprisals against fellow Muslims who would not cooperate with them.

Beginning in 1956 and continuing until the summer of 1957, the FLN attempted to paralyze the administration of Algiers through what has come to be known as the Battle of Algiers. Attacks by the FLN against both military and civilian European targets were countered by paratroopers led by General Jacques Massu. To stem the tide of FLN attacks, the French military resorted to the torture and summary execution of hundreds of suspects. The entire leadership of the FLN was eventually eliminated or forced to flee.

The French also cut Algeria off from independent Tunisia and Morocco by erecting barbed-wire fences that were illuminated at night by searchlights. This separated the Algerian resistance bands within the country from some 30,000 armed Algerians who occupied positions between the fortified fences and the actual frontiers of Tunisia and Morocco, from which they drew supplies.

In September 1958, the FLN formed the Provisional Government of the Algerian Republic (Gouvernement Provisionel de la République Algérienne; GPRA), initially headed by Ferhat Abbas. That same month, French Prime Minister de Gaulle publicly declared that the Algerians had the right to determine their own future. The settler population responded by staging uprisings in both 1960 and 1961, neither of which were successful.

Negotiations between France and the GPRA started in May 1961 but were broken off in July, after which Abbas was replaced as premier by the much younger Benyoussef Ben Khedda. Settler opposition meanwhile coalesced around a body calling itself the Secret Army Organization (Organisation de l'Armée Secrète; OAS), which began to employ random acts of terror in an effort to disrupt peace negotiations. Negotiations resumed the following March, and an agreement was finally reached. Algeria would become independent, provided that a referendum confirmed the desire for it. French aid would continue, and Europeans could depart, remain as foreigners, or take Algerian citizenship. This announcement produced a violent outburst of terrorism, but in May it subsided as it became obvious that such actions were futile. A referendum held in Algeria in July 1962 recorded some 6,000,000 votes in favour of independence and only 16,000 against. After three days of continuous Algerian rejoicing, the GPRA entered Algiers in triumph as many Europeans prepared to depart.

INDEPENDENT ALGERIA

The human cost of the war remains unknown, particularly on the Algerian side. Some estimates put French military losses at 27,000 killed and civilian losses at 5,000 to 6,000. French sources suggest that casualties among Algerians totaled between 300,000 and 500,000, while Algerian sources claim as many as 1,500,000.

Scores of villages were destroyed; forests were widely damaged; and some 2,000,000 inhabitants were moved to new settlements. The Europeans who left Algeria at the time of independence constituted the great majority of senior administrators and managerial and technical experts, yet many public services remained functional; only some 10,000 French teachers remained, often in isolated posts.

With the loss of management on farms and in factories, however, production fell, while unemployment and underemployment reached extreme levels. The mass exodus of the French left the new government with vast abandoned lands. These and the remaining French estates (all French land had been nationalized by 1963) were turned into state farms run by worker committees, which began to produce export crops, notably wine.

Political life was particularly contentious following independence. The leadership of Ben Khedda, the president of the GPRA, was upset by the release from French custody of five GPRA leaders, including Ben Bella. Soon the heads of the provisional government—and, more decisively, the army commanders—split. Houari Boumedienne and his powerful frontier army sided with Ben Bella, who had formed the Political Bureau to challenge the power of the GPRA. Other dominant figures sided with Ben Khedda, while the commanders of the internal guerrillas, who had led the war, opposed all external factions, both military and civilian. Mounting tension and localized military clashes threatened an all-out civil war. The spontaneous demonstrations of a population weary of nearly eight years of war with France interceded between the military factions and saved the country from sliding into more warfare.

Through delicate political maneuvering, Ben Bella and the Political Bureau were able to draw up the list of candidates for the National People's Assembly, which was ratified in September 1962 by an overwhelming majority of the electorate. The new assembly asked Ben Bella to form the new nation's first government.

With the military support of Boumedienne, Ben Bella asserted his power, fighting a localized armed rebellion led by fellow rebel leader Aït-Ahmed and Colonel Mohand ou el-Hadj in Great Kabylia. Because Ben Bella's personal style of government and his reckless promises of support for revolutionary movements were not conducive to orderly administration, there were also serious divisions within the ruling group. Following vicious political infighting in April 1963, Political Bureau member and FLN secretary-general Khider left the country, taking a large amount of party funds with him. He was assassinated in Madrid several years later. Other dissident leaders were also gradually eliminated, and this left control securely in the hands of Ben Bella and the army commander Boumedienne. Ben Bella's apparent plan to remove Boumedienne and his supporters was foiled in June 1965 when Boumedienne and the army moved first. Ben Bella's erratic political style and poor administrative record made his removal acceptable to Algerians, but the Boumedienne regime began with little popular support.

In the following years Boumedienne moved undramatically but effectively to consolidate his power, with army loyalty remaining the basic element. Efforts to reorganize the FLN met with some success. Boumedienne's cautious and deliberate approach was apparent in constitutional developments as communal elections were held in 1967 and provincial elections in 1969. Elections for the National People's Assembly, however, did not first take place until 1977.

TUNISIA

Tunisia's security was directly threatened in 1835, when the Ottoman Empire deposed the ruling dynasty in Libya and reestablished direct Ottoman rule. Thereafter, the vulnerable *beylik* of Tunis found itself surrounded by two larger powers—France and the Ottoman Empire—both of which had designs on Tunisia. From that time until the establishment of the French protectorate in 1881, Tunisian rulers had to placate the larger powers while working to strengthen the state from within.

The final collapse of the Tunisian *beylik* came during the reign of Muḥammad al-Ṣādiq (1859–82).

Though sympathetic to the need for reforms, Muḥammad was too weak either to control his own government or to keep the European powers at bay. He did, in 1861, proclaim the first constitution (*dustūr*; also *destour*) in the Arabic-speaking world, but this step toward representative government was cut short by runaway debt, a problem exacerbated by the government's practice of securing loans from European bankers at exorbitant rates.

When the principal minister, Muṣṭafā Khaznadār (who had served from the earliest days of Aḥmad Bey's reign), attempted to squeeze more taxes out of the hard-pressed peasants, the countryside rose in a revolt (1864). This uprising almost overthrew the regime, but the government ultimately suppressed it through a combination of guile and brutality.

Though Tunisia went bankrupt in 1869 and an international financial commission—with British, French, and Italian representatives—was imposed on the country, there was one last attempt to reform Tunisia from within and thus avoid complete European domination. It was made during the reformist ministry of Khayr al-Dīn (1873–77), one of the most effective statesmen of the 19th-century Muslim world. However, enemies from within and European intrigues from without conspired to force him from office. The final blow to Tunisia's sovereignty came at the Congress of Berlin in 1878, when Britain acquiesced to France's control of Tunisia.

On the pretext that Tunisians had encroached on Algerian territory, France invaded Tunisia in 1881 and imposed the Treaty of Bardo, which sanctioned French military occupation of Tunisia, transferred to France the bey's authority over finance and foreign relations, and provided for the appointment of a French resident minister as intermediary in all matters of common interest. This provoked an uprising in southern Tunisia during which France attacked and captured Sousse in July 1881, took Kairouan in October, and seized Gafsa and Gabès in November. After the death of Muḥammad al-Ṣādiq, his successor, ʿAlī, was forced to introduce administrative, judicial, and financial reforms that the French government considered useful. This agreement, known as the Convention of Al-Marsa, was signed in 1883 and solidified French control over Tunisia.

THE PROTECTORATE

Tunisia became a protectorate of France by treaty rather than by outright conquest, as was the case in Algeria. Officially, the bey remained an absolute monarch: Tunisian ministers were still appointed, the government structure was preserved, and

Tunisians continued to be subjects of the bey. The French did not confiscate land, convert mosques into churches, or change the official language. Nevertheless, supreme authority was passed to the French resident general.

Under French guidance, Tunisia's finances were soon stabilized and modern communications established. Though France never overtly seized land or displaced the population, as had occurred in Algeria, the most fertile portions of northern Tunisia, comprising the Majardah valley and the Sharīk Peninsula, were passed on to other European countries. Valuable phosphate mines began operating near Gafsa in the south, and vegetables were cultivated and exported from the Majardah valley after French and Italian colonists had become established there.

By the 1890s a small French-educated group—the members of which came to be called "Young Tunisians"—began pushing for both modernizing reforms based on a European model and greater participation by Tunisians in their own government. The group's conduct during the protectorate, however, was cautious and reserved. Their major weapon became *Le Tunisien*, a French-language newspaper founded in 1907. With the printing of an Arabic edition in 1909, the Young Tunisians simultaneously educated their compatriots and persuaded the more liberal French to help move Tunisia toward modernity.

Even this moderate protonationalism was subject to repressive measures by the French in 1911–12. Little nationalist activity took place during World War I (1914–18), but the first attempt at mass political organization came during the interwar period, when the Destour (Constitution) Party was created (the party was named for the short-lived Tunisian constitution of 1861). In 1920 the Destour Party presented the bey and the French government with a document that demanded that a constitutional form of government be established in which Tunisians would possess the same rights as Europeans. The immediate result was the arrest of ʿAbd al-ʿAzīz al-Thaʿālibī, the Destour leader. Two years later the aged bey, Muḥammad al-Nāṣir, requested that the program of the Destour be adopted or he would abdicate. In response, the resident general, Lucien Saint, surrounded the bey's palace with troops, and the demand was withdrawn. Saint thus introduced restrictive measures, together with minor reforms, that pacified Tunisian sentiment and weakened the nationalist movement for several years.

In 1934 the young Tunisian lawyer Habib Bourguiba and his colleagues broke with the Destour Party to form a new organization, the

This photo of Habib Bourguiba dates from 1938. He would go on to become the architect of Tunisia's independence and one of the major voices of moderation and gradualism in the Arab world.

Neo-Destour, which aimed at spreading propaganda and gaining mass support. Under Bourguiba's vigorous leadership, the new party soon supplanted the existing Destour Party and its leaders. Attempts by the French to suppress the new movement only fueled the fire. The Neo-Destour began to gain more power and influence after the arrival of the Popular Front government in France in 1936. When the Popular Front government collapsed, repression was renewed in Tunisia and was met with civil disobedience. In 1938 serious disturbances led to the arrest of Bourguiba and other leaders of the party, which was then officially dissolved.

WORLD WAR II AND INDEPENDENCE

At the outbreak of war in 1939, Neo-Destour leaders were deported to France. Following the German occupation of Vichy France, Hitler handed them over to the Italians, as he regarded Tunisia as a sphere of Italian influence. The fascists hoped to gain support for the Axis, but Bourguiba refused to cooperate. In March 1943 he made a noncommittal broadcast, and the Neo-Destour leaders were finally allowed to proceed to Tunis, where the reigning bey, Muḥammad al-Munṣif (Moncef), formed a ministry of individuals who were sympathetic to Destour.

The assumption of power by the Free French after the Nazi retreat produced complete disillusionment for the Neo-Destour cause. The bey was deposed, while Bourguiba, accused of collaboration with the Nazis, escaped imprisonment by fleeing in disguise to Egypt in 1945. Still, a vigorous campaign of propaganda for Tunisian independence continued, and, in view of the emancipation of the eastern Arab states and later of neighbouring Libya, the French felt compelled to make concessions. In 1951 the French permitted a government with nationalist sympathies to take office—of which the secretary-general of the Neo-Destour, Salah Ben Youssef, became a member—and Bourguiba was allowed to return to Tunisia. When the newly formed government wished to establish a Tunisian parliament, however, further repressions ensued. Bourguiba was exiled, and most of the ministers were put under arrest. This resulted, for the first time, in outbreaks of terrorism. Nationalist guerrillas began to operate in the mountains, virtually paralyzing the country.

In July 1954 the French premier, Pierre Mendès-France, promised to grant complete autonomy to Tunisia, subject to a negotiated agreement.

Bourguiba returned to Tunisia and was able to supervise the negotiations without directly participating. In June 1955 an agreement was finally signed by the Tunisian delegates—though it imposed strict limits in the fields of foreign policy, education, defense, and finance—and a mainly Neo-Destour ministry was formed. Salah Ben Youssef denounced the document, saying it was too restrictive, and refused to attend a specially summoned congress that unanimously supported Bourguiba. In response, he organized a brief armed resistance in the south that was quickly repressed. Ben Youssef fled the country to escape imprisonment; he was assassinated in 1961.

The French granted full independence to Tunisia in an accord that was reached on March 20, 1956, and Bourguiba was chosen prime minister. The rule of the beys was subsequently abolished, and on July 25, 1957, a republic was declared, with Bourguiba as president.

LIBYA

Part of the Ottoman Empire from the early 16th century, Libya experienced autonomous rule (analogous to that in Ottoman Algeria and Tunisia) under the Karamanli dynasty from 1711 to 1835. For the next 77 years the area was administered by officials from the Ottoman capital of Constantinople (present-day Istanbul) and shared in the limited modernization common to the rest of the empire. In 1911, however, the Italians, who had banking and other interests in the country, launched an invasion.

The Ottomans sued for peace in 1912, but Italy found it more difficult to subdue the local population. Resistance to the Italian occupation continued throughout World War I. After the war Italy considered coming to terms with nationalist forces in Tripolitania and with the Sanūsiyyah, which was strong in Cyrenaica. These negotiations foundered, however, and the arrival of a strong governor, Giuseppe Volpi, in Libya and a Fascist government in Italy (1922) inaugurated an Italian policy of thorough colonization. The coastal areas of Tripolitania were subdued by 1923, but in Cyrenaica Sanūsī resistance, led by ʿUmar al-Mukhtār, continued until his capture and execution in 1931.

ITALIAN COLONIZATION

In the 1920s and ʾ30s the Italian government expended large sums on developing towns, roads, and agricultural colonies for Italian settlers. The most ambitious effort was the program of Italian immigration called "demographic colonization," launched

by the Fascist leader Benito Mussolini in 1935. As
a result of these efforts, by the outbreak of World
War II, some 150,000 Italians had settled in Libya
and constituted roughly one-fifth of that country's
total population.

These colonizing efforts and the resulting economic development of Libya were largely destroyed
during the North Africa campaigns of 1941–43.
Cyrenaica changed hands three times, and by the end
of 1942 all of the Italian settlers had left. Cyrenaica
largely reverted to pastoralism. Economic and administrative development fostered by Italy survived
in Tripolitania; however, Libya by 1945 was impoverished, underpopulated, and also divided into regions—Tripolitania, Cyrenaica, and Fezzan—of differing political, economic, and religious traditions.

INDEPENDENCE

The future of Libya gave rise to long discussions after
the war. In view of the contribution to the fighting
made by a volunteer Sanūsī force, the British foreign
minister pledged in 1942 that the Sanūsīs would not
again be subjected to Italian rule. During the discussions, which lasted four years, suggestions included
an Italian trusteeship, a United Nations (UN) trusteeship, a Soviet mandate for Tripolitania, and various

Libya's first king, Sīdī Muḥammad Idrīs al-Mahdī al-Sanūsī, is often just know as Idris I. He ruled Libya until he was overthrown in 1969.

compromises. Finally, in November 1949, the UN General Assembly voted that Libya should become a united and independent kingdom no later than January 1, 1952.

A constitution creating a federal state with a separate parliament for each province was drawn up, and the pro-British head of the Sanūsiyyah, Sīdī Muḥammad Idrīs al-Mahdī al-Sanūsī, was chosen king by a national assembly in 1950. On December 24, 1951, King Idris I declared the country independent. Political parties were prohibited, and the king's authority was sovereign. Though not themselves Sanūsīs, the Tripolitanians accepted the monarchy largely in order to profit from the British promise that the Sanūsīs would not again be subjected to Italian rule. King Idris, however, showed a marked preference for living in Cyrenaica, where he built a new capital on the site of the Sanūsī *zāwiyah* at Al-Bayḍā'. Though Libya joined the Arab League in 1953 and in 1956 refused British troops permission to land during the Suez Crisis, the government in general adopted a pro-Western position in international affairs.

MOROCCO

By the later part of the 19th century, the sultan of Morocco was trapped between the European demands for free trade, conceded in 1856, and an unruly tribal population that resisted the imposition of a central government. Although defeated by France at the Battle of Isly in 1844 and by Spain at Tetuan (Tétouan) in 1860, Morocco was nevertheless able to rely on the support of Great Britain in its dealings with Europe. As a result—although Morocco's immigrant Europeans in this period conducted themselves with impunity under the protection of their consuls—the sultans Muḥammad and Hassan, who ruled Morocco from 1859 to 1894, maintained the country's independence and gradually extended a network of *caids* (*qā'ids*), or district governors, into the far south of the country. At the beginning of the 20th century—after the fall of Tunisia to French control in 1881—Morocco was the sole exception to colonial rule in North Africa.

The Western powers met with Moroccan representatives at Algeciras, Spain, in 1906, to discuss the
country's future. The Algeciras Conference confirmed
the integrity of the sultan's domains but sanctioned
French and Spanish policing Moroccan ports and
collecting the customs dues. In 1909, Mawlāy ʿAbd
al-Ḥāfiẓ led a rebellion and replaced his brother as
sultan. Disorder increased until, besieged by
tribesmen in Fès, he was forced to ask the French to
rescue him. When they had done so, he had no choice
but to sign the Treaty of Fez (March 30, 1912), by
which Morocco became a French protectorate. In
return, the French guaranteed that the status of the
sultan and his successors would be maintained.
Provision was also made to meet the Spanish claim
for a special position in the north of the country.
Tangier, long the seat of the diplomatic missions,
retained a separate administration.

THE FRENCH PROTECTORATE

The French took their protectorate over Tunisia
as the model for their Moroccan policy. There
were, however, important differences. First, the
protectorate was established only two years before
the outbreak of World War I, which brought with
it a new attitude toward colonial rule. Second,

Morocco had a thousand-year tradition of independence. Though it had been strongly influenced by the civilization of Muslim Spain, it had never been subject to Ottoman rule. These circumstances and the proximity of Morocco to Spain created a special relationship between the two countries.

Morocco was also unique among the countries of North Africa in possessing a coast on the Atlantic, in the rights that various nations derived from the Act of Algeciras, and in the privileges that their diplomatic missions had acquired in Tangier. Thus, the northern tenth of the country, with both Atlantic and Mediterranean coasts, together with the desert province of Tarfaya in the southwest adjoining the Spanish Sahara, were excluded from the French-controlled area and treated as a Spanish protectorate. In the French zone, the fiction of the sultan's sovereignty was maintained, but the French-appointed resident general held the real authority and was subject only to the approval of the government in Paris. The sultan worked through newly created departments staffed by French officials. The negligible role that the Moroccan government (*makhzan*) actually played can be seen by the fact that Muḥammad al-Muqrī, the grand vizier when the protectorate was installed, held the same post when Morocco recovered its independence 44 years later; he was by then more than 100 years old. As in Tunisia, country districts were administered by *contrôleurs civils*, except in certain areas such as Fès, where it was felt that officers of the rank of general should supervise the administration. In the south certain Amazigh chiefs (*qāʾids*), of whom the best known was Thami al-Glaoui, were given a great deal of independence.

The first resident general, General (later Marshal) Louis-Hubert-Gonzalve Lyautey, possessed a deep appreciation of Moroccan civilization. His idea was to leave the Moroccan elite intact and rule through a policy of cooptation. A new administrative capital was created on the Atlantic coast at Rabat, and a commercial port subsequently was developed at Casablanca. Lyautey's plan to build new European cities separate from the old Moroccan towns left the traditional medinas intact.

As early as 1920 Lyautey had submitted a report saying that "a young generation is growing up which is full of life and needs activity....Lacking the outlets which our administration offers only sparingly and in subordinate positions they will find an alternative way out." Only six years after Lyautey's report, young Moroccans both in Rabat, the new administrative capital, and in Fès, the centre of traditional Arab-Islamic learning and culture, were meeting independently of one another to discuss demands for reforms within the terms of the protectorate treaty. They asked for more schools, a new judicial system, and the abolition of the regime of the Amazigh *qā'ids* in the south, study missions in France and the Middle East, and the cessation of official colonization.

Also significant was the French attempt to use the differences between Arabs and Imazighen to undercut any growing sense of national unity. This led the French to issue the Berber Decree in 1930, which was a crude effort to divide Imazighen and Arabs. The result was just the opposite of French intentions. It provoked a Moroccan nationalist reaction and forced the administration to modify its proposals.

At the outbreak of World War II in 1939, sultan Sīdī Muḥammad Ben Yūsuf (later Muhammad V) issued a call for cooperation with the French, and a large Moroccan contingent served with distinction in France. After the fall of France in 1940, the sultan signified his independence by refusing to approve anti-Jewish legislation. When Anglo-American troops landed in 1942, he refused to retire to the interior. The arrival of U.S. and British troops exposed Moroccans to the outside world to an unprecedented degree. Allied and Axis radio propaganda, which called for Moroccan independence, strongly attracted

Arab listeners. Amid these circumstances, the nationalist movement took the new title of Ḥizb al-Istiqlāl (Independence Party). After the party submitted a memorandum asking for independence under a constitutional regime in January 1944, nationalist leaders (including Aḥmad Balafrej, secretary general of the Istiqlāl) were unjustly accused and arrested for collaborating with the Nazis. This caused rioting in Fès and elsewhere. Soon after, the sultan made an official state visit to Tangier, where he made a speech emphasizing his country's links with the Arab world, omitting the expected flattering reference to the French protectorate.

In 1951 the French encouraged a tribal rebellion against the sultan, and, on the pretext of protecting him, they surrounded his palace with troops. Under these conditions he was induced to denounce the nationalist movement. In August 1953 the French deported the sultan. In November 1954 the French position was further complicated by the outbreak of the Algerian war for independence. Meanwhile, a guerrilla liberation army began to operate against French posts near the Spanish Zone.

In October Thami al-Glaoui declared publicly that only the restoration of Muḥammad V could restore harmony. The French government agreed to allow the sultan to form a constitutional government for Morocco, and Sīdī Muḥammad returned to Rabat in November. On March 2, 1956, independence was proclaimed. The sultan formed a government that included representation from various elements of the indigenous population, while the governmental departments formerly headed by French officials became ministries headed by Moroccans.

THE SPANISH ZONE

Spain appointed a *khalīfah*, or viceroy, chosen from the Moroccan royal family as nominal head of state and provided him with a puppet Moroccan government. This enabled Spain to conduct affairs independently of the French Zone while nominally preserving Moroccan unity. Tangier, though it had a Spanish-speaking population of 40,000, received a special international administration under a *mandūb*, or a representative of the sultan. In reality the *mandūb* was chosen by the French. Spanish troops occupied Tangier after the defeat of France in 1940 but withdrew after the Allied victory in 1945.

The Spanish Zone surrounded the ports of Ceuta and Melilla, which Spain had held for centuries, and included the iron mines of the Rif Mountains. The Spanish selected Tétouan for their capital. As in the French Zone, European-staffed departments were created, while the rural districts were administered by *interventores*, corresponding to the French *contrôleurs civils*. The first area to be occupied was on the plain, facing the Atlantic, that included the towns of Larache, Ksar el-Kebir, and Asilah. That area was the stronghold of the former Moroccan governor Aḥmad al-Raisūnī (Raisūlī), who was half patriot and half brigand. The Spanish government found it difficult to tolerate his independence; in March 1913 al-Raisūnī retired into a refuge in the mountains, where he remained until his capture 12 years later by another Moroccan leader, Abd el-Krim.

Abd el-Krim was an Amazigh who had a knowledge of both the Arabic and Spanish languages and ways of life. Imprisoned after World War I for his subversive activities, he later went to Ajdir in the Rif Mountains to plan an uprising. In July 1921 Abd el-Krim destroyed a Spanish force sent against him and subsequently established the Republic of the Rif, which was formally constituted as an independent state in 1923. It took a combined French and Spanish force numbering more than 250,000 troops before he was defeated.

The remainder of the period of the Spanish protectorate was relatively calm. In 1936, General Francisco Franco was able to launch his attack on the Spanish Republic from Morocco and to enroll a

A skilled tactician and capable organizer, Abd el-Krim led a liberation movement that made him the hero of the Maghrib.

large number of Moroccan volunteers, who served him loyally in the Spanish Civil War. Though the Spanish had fewer resources than the French, their regime was in some respects more liberal and less subject to ethnic discrimination. The language of instruction in the schools was Arabic rather than Spanish, and Moroccan students were encouraged to go to Egypt for a Muslim education. There was no attempt to set Amazigh against Arab as in the French Zone, but this might have been the result of the introduction of Muslim law by Abd el-Krim. After the Republic of the Rif was suppressed, there was little cooperation between the two protecting powers. Their disagreement reached a new intensity in 1953 when the French deposed and deported the sultan. The Spanish high commissioner, who had not been consulted, refused to recognize this action. Nationalists forced to leave the French area used the Spanish Zone as a refuge.

The Spanish authorities were taken by surprise when the French decided to grant independence to Morocco in 1956. A corresponding agreement with the Spanish was nevertheless reached on April 7, 1956, and was marked by a visit of the sultan to Spain. The Spanish protectorate was thus brought to an end without the troubles that marked the termination of French control. With the end of

the Spanish protectorate and the withdrawal of the
Spanish high commissioner, the Moroccan *khalīfah*,
and other officials from Tétouan, the city again became a quiet, provincial capital. The introduction of
the Moroccan franc to replace the peseta as currency,
however, caused a great rise in the cost of living
in the former Spanish area, along with difficulties
brought on by the introduction of French-speaking
Moroccan officials. In 1958–59 these changes generated disorders in the Rif region. Tangier, too, lost
much of the superficial brilliance it had developed as
a separate zone. As in the former French Zone, many
European and Jewish inhabitants left. The southern
protectorate area of Tarfaya was handed back to Morocco in 1958, while the Spanish unconditionally gave
up Ifni in 1970, hoping to gain recognition of their
rights to Melilla and Ceuta.

CHAPTER TWO

WESTERN AFRICA

• •

Western Africa—comprising the countries of Benin, Burkina Faso, Cameroon, Cabo Verde, Côte d'Ivoire, Equatorial Guinea, The Gambia, Ghana, Guinea, Guinea-Bissau, Liberia, Mali, Mauritania, Niger, Nigeria, Senegal, Sierra Leone, and Togo—may be divided into several broad physiographic regions. The northern portion is composed of a broad band of semiarid terrain, called the western Sudan, stretching from the Atlantic Ocean on the west to the area of Lake Chad on the east. It borders the Sahara (desert) on the north and the Guinea Coast forests, which flourish along the Atlantic coast, to the south.

Culturally, the people of the region belong for the most part to one of three major language families. In the northern and least-populous Saharan regions, Arabs and Imazighen of the Afro-Asiatic language family predominate. South of a line connecting the course of the Sénégal River, the Niger River, and the southern two-thirds of Nigeria, Niger-Congo languages are spoken. Along the middle course of the Niger River and around Lake Chad, Nilo-Saharan languages related to those of peoples farther east predominate. These peoples are divided into a very complex ethnic mosaic but may often be classified by their individual languages.

Before the race for partition, only three European powers—France, Portugal, and Britain—had territory in tropical Africa, located mainly in western Africa. Once conditions were ripe for the introduction of railroads and steamships in West Africa, tensions between the English and French increased as each country tried to extend its sphere of influence. As customs duties, the prime source of colonial revenue, could be evaded in uncontrolled ports, both powers began to stretch their coastal frontiers, and overlapping claims and disputes soon arose. The commercial penetration of the interior created additional rivalry and set off a chain reaction. The drive for exclusive control over interior areas intensified in response to both economic competition and the need for protection from African states resisting foreign intrusion. This drive for African possessions was intensified by the new entrants to the colonial race who felt menaced by the possibility of being completely locked out.

EARLY INTERACTIONS WITH EUROPEANS

The arrival of European sea traders at the Guinea coastlands in the 15th century clearly marks a new epoch in their history and in the history of all of western Africa. The pioneers were the Portuguese. Their main goal was to reach Asia by circumnavigating Africa, but they also hoped to divert some of the trans-Saharan gold trade from Muslim North Africa to Christian Europe.

The most momentous discovery in western Africa came in 1471, when Portuguese captains first reached the coast of modern Ghana between the mouths of the Ankobra and Volta rivers. It was quickly appreciated that the Akan peoples of this coast had access to supplies of gold and that they were willing and organized to trade some of this gold for base metals, cloth, and other manufactures. The Portuguese called this coast Mina, "the mine," while in European languages generally it became known as the Gold Coast. Portugal's general strategy in western Africa was to keep territorial and administrative commitments to the minimum necessary to

The Portuguese built Elmina Castle in 1482. The fort was later taken over by the Dutch, and then the English. It played a major role in the slave trade. Tens of thousands of Africans were imprisoned in its dungeons.

develop and benefit Portuguese commercial activities that were already in existence.

THE ATLANTIC SLAVE TRADE

At roughly the same time Portugal was establishing footholds in West Africa, it and other European powers were establishing colonies in the Americas. Plantation agriculture in the tropics required large, regular supplies of cheap labour. America did not have these, but, just across the Atlantic, western Africa seemed to have relatively great quantities of productive labour. As early as the 1440s, the Portuguese had begun to transport some African slaves to supplement the meagre labour resources of their own country, as well as their own plantations in Madeira, the Cape Verde Islands, and the islands of the Gulf of Guinea. The Spaniards, and subsequently other Europeans, in America thus naturally came to look to Africa to make good their labour shortage, and a slave trade to the Caribbean had commenced on a small scale in the 1520s.

By the time the Dutch West India Company entered the scene in the mid-1620s, in all probability about 400,000 slaves had been imported into the Americas, and the annual volume of imports had risen to about 10,000 a year. To ensure its sources of supply, the Dutch company embarked on the conquest of the Portuguese bases on the western African shores. By the 1660s probably as many as 15,000 African slaves were being landed in the Americas each year. The Dutch West India Company's activities in the Atlantic slave trade aroused interest throughout the ports of northwestern Europe, and soon merchants from France, Britain, Germany, and Scandinavia, as well as private Dutch traders, were competing with the Dutch company. French and British competition soon became of major importance.

The peak of the Atlantic slave trade seems to have been reached in the 1780s, when on average some 78,000 slaves were brought to the Americas each year. However a fair proportion of these slaves never reached the other side of the Atlantic because of deaths from disease, maltreatment, or maritime disaster.

In the first decades of the 19th century, social pressures in Europe brought about the abolition of the slave trade. Britain, which outlawed the slave trade in 1807, took the lead in stamping it out. British ships had been by far the largest carriers of slaves at the end of the 18th century, and only Britain really possessed the naval resources necessary to secure enforcement of anti-slave-trade laws on the high seas. Economic interest combined with abstract morality to induce successive British governments to bring pressure on other governments to outlaw their slave trades and to permit the British navy to help enforce their laws on their ships at sea.

THE GUINEA COASTLANDS AND THE EUROPEANS (1807–79)

Along with a substantial naval presence in western Africa, Britain also acquired new political, commercial, and missionary presences. These led to increasing interference in the domestic affairs of African societies and their governments. For the greater part of the 19th century the prime centre for British naval, political, and missionary activities on the western African coast was Sierra Leone. Toward the end of the 18th century the Sierra Leone peninsula had been chosen by British philanthropists as a suitable place to which Africans who had been taken to Britain as slaves and freed there, or who had fought on the British side in the American Revolution, might be repatriated. A first group was sent out and settled on the site of the future Freetown in 1787.

The most prosperous British trade, though, developed in the Niger delta. British shipping had been paramount there when the British slave trade had been abolished in 1807, and the merchants of the delta city-states had quickly adapted themselves to offering palm oil as an alternative export to slaves. Britain's Industrial Revolution had occasioned a growing demand for vegetable oils as lubricants and for the manufacture of soap, and about nine-tenths of this trade was initially with that region.

By the middle of the century the development of the liberated African community in Sierra Leone under the tutelage of British administration, churches, and education meant that some of its members were providing a considerable reinforcement for the British interest in western Africa. Economic activities in Sierra Leone itself were limited, and Sierra Leoneans were soon finding their way along the coast as independent pioneers of trade and Westernization or as auxiliaries to British traders, officials, and missionaries. Their most significant influence was in Yorubaland. By the 1840s at least half the liberated Africans were of Yoruba extraction, and by this time their homeland afforded considerable scope both for independent traders and for people seeking to introduce Christian and Western ideas and ways into African life. Both these circumstances derived from the failure of the Oyo empire in the 18th century to establish a stable form of central government capable of maintaining a firm control over the provinces it had conquered. There remained a dangerously uncertain balance of power between the king and the traditional chiefs of the capital.

The first serious advance of British power in western Africa occurred on the Gold Coast. After the withdrawal of British officials and troops in 1828, the British Gold Coast traders took on a young army officer, George Maclean, to represent their interests there. Maclean negotiated a peace with Asante and established an informal jurisdiction through the coastal states, which brought security

for both British and Asante merchants. The conse-
quent fourfold increase in British trade combined
with the uncertain legal status of Maclean's jurisdiction to bring British officials back to the forts in
1843. In 1850 they took over the Danish forts also,
but the continued Dutch presence on the coast prevented them from raising an effective revenue from
customs duties, and they quarreled with the coastal
peoples over the issue of direct taxation.

African sovereignty had also been infringed
between Sierra Leone and the Ivory Coast where,
inspired by the Sierra Leone example, private U.S
organizations had settled freed slaves for whom
there was no place in their own society prior to 1863.
British and French merchants questioned the right of
the settlers to control and to tax their trade and, since
formal U.S. policy was anticolonial, the result, in
1847, was the proclamation of the Republic of
Liberia. The settler government then embarked on
a long struggle to assert control over the local Africans. Because, unlike a colonial government, it had
no metropolitan resources or finance to help, this
was a prolonged business.

The growth of British trade, and of British influence and power, in western Africa was by no means
to the liking of the government, traders, and navy
of France—Britain's principal competitors in the

previous century. But France's mercantile interest in western Africa was not as strong as Britain's, and its traders there received less official and naval support than did the British. Not until the 1870s and the opening of the European scramble was any serious effort made to develop the trading footholds that were established on the coast between Senegal and Sierra Leone, on the Ivory Coast, and between the Gold Coast and Lagos.

France's main effort in western Africa was devoted to developing its old interests in Senegal following the British withdrawal in 1817. Initially an attempt was made to replace the former business of exporting labour to the West Indies by developing a local plantation economy. By the 1820s this was foundering, and matters then drifted until the arrival in 1854 of a new governor, Louis Faidherbe, a soldier with experience in the conquest of Algeria and in the government of its peoples. Faidherbe's concept was to secure control of the exports of the westernmost Sudan by extending French military and political control up the Sénégal River and to encourage local African production of the peanut (groundnut) to help meet the growing French and European demand for vegetable oils. By the time of his departure in 1865, Senegal had become the prototype for subsequent European colonization in western Africa and a springboard from which the French could think of conquering the whole Sudan.

COLONIZATION

The European scramble to partition and occupy African territory is often treated as a peripheral aspect of the political and economic rivalries that developed between the new industrial nations in Europe itself and that were particularly acute from about 1870 to 1914. In western Africa, however, it seems fair to say that the beginnings of the scramble and partition were evident at least a generation before the 1880s and that they were determined by the local situation as much as or more than they were by European domestic rivalries. Already during 1854–74, the logic of the situation in western Africa had led France and Britain to take the political initiatives of creating formal European colonies in Senegal, in Lagos, and in the Gold Coast. All along the coast, in fact, the traditional African political order was becoming ineffective in the face of European economic and social pressures. For most of the 19th century these pressures had been predominantly British, but in the 1870s French companies began to offer effective competition to the British traders not only in Upper Guinea, where they had always been strong, but also on the Ivory Coast, in the ports immediately to the west of Lagos, and even in the lower river and delta of the Niger. An unstable situation was developing in which the European traders were likely to call for further intervention and support from their governments, and especially so if the terms of trade were to turn against them. Low world prices for primary produce during the depression years from the 1870s to the mid-1890s certainly caused difficulties for Europeans trading to western Africa and led them to think that an increase in European control there would enable them to secure its produce more cheaply.

The changing balance of power in western Africa was not confined to the coastlands. By the 1870s formal French and British armies had already ventured into the interior and had inflicted defeats on such major African powers as those of al-Ḥājj ʿUmar and Asante. In 1879 Faidherbe's heirs on the Sénégal River had launched the thrust that was to take French arms conquering eastward across the Sudan to Lake Chad and beyond. By the end of the 1870s France and Britain, therefore, were already on the march in western Africa. The principal effect of the new forces stemming from domestic power rivalries in Europe itself—the most dramatic of which was the appearance in 1884 of the German flag on the Togoland coast, between the Gold Coast and

Dahomey, and in the Cameroons—was to intensify and to accelerate existing French and British tendencies to exert their political and military authority at the expense of traditional African rulers.

FRENCH AREAS OF INTEREST

There can be no question but that, by the end of the 1870s, the advance of the British interest in western Africa had been more rewarding than the advance of the French interest. Devoting their attention primarily to the active economies of the Niger delta, the Lagos hinterland, and the Gold Coast, British traders had secured $24 million of business a year, compared with the French merchants' trade of $8 million, three-quarters of which was concentrated on the Sénégal River. Initially, therefore, the French had much more incentive for expansion than the British.

Britain was already in political control of the Gold Coast, and the arrival of the German treaty makers in Togo and in the Cameroons in 1884 hastened it to declare its protectorate over most of the intervening coastline on which British traders were active. The gap left between Lagos and Togo was swiftly filled by the French, and from 1886 they also established formal authority over all other parts of the coastline that were not already claimed by the governments of Liberia, Portugal, or Britain. In this way the baselines were established from which France subsequently developed the colonies of Dahomey, the Ivory Coast, and French Guinea.

France's advance inland from these southern coasts was subsidiary, however, to the main thrust, which was eastward from the Sénégal region through the Sudan. The glamour of its past had persuaded the French that the Sudan was the most advanced, most populated, and most productive zone of western Africa. Once they had reached the upper Niger from the Sénégal (1879–83), the French forces had a highway permitting them further rapid advances. By 1896 they had linked up with the troops that had conquered Dahomey (1893–94) to threaten the lower Niger territories, which British traders had penetrated from the delta.

French claims to sovereignty over what is now Mauritania were regularly disputed by the leaders (referred to as "amirs" or "commanders" by the French) of the region. The French entered into treaty relations with the amirs in 1858, but France made little effort to exert control over southern Mauritania until the opening years of the 20th century. The "pacification" of Mauritania, as it was styled by the French military, continued until 1912, and the final battle to subdue a Reguibat band took place in 1934. The French nickname for the colony was "Le Grand Vide" ("the great void"); so long as the population was quiet there was little evidence of a French presence.

BRITISH AREAS OF INTEREST

The rapid French advance across western Africa from the Sénégal River had denied the British any chance of exploiting the commercial hinterland of the Gambia River and had severely restricted their opportunities from Sierra Leone. Government and mercantile interests nonetheless were able to agree on the need for British action to keep the French (and also the Germans from Togo and from the Cameroons) out of the hinterlands of the Gold Coast, Lagos, and the Niger delta. Asante submitted to an ultimatum in 1896 (the real war of conquest was delayed until 1900–01, when the British had to suppress a widespread rebellion against their authority), and a British protectorate was extended northward to the limits of Asante influence.

On the Niger, British interests were first maintained by an amalgamation of trading companies formed in 1879 by Sir George Goldie to combat French commercial competition. In 1897 the British government agreed to support Goldie's Royal Niger

Company in the development of military forces. Three years later, however, it recognized the foolishness of allowing the company's servants and soldiers to compete for African territory with French government officials and troops and to enforce its monopolistic policies on all other traders within its sphere. The company was divested of its political role, and the British government itself took over direct responsi-

George Goldie was responsible for the development of northern Nigeria into an orderly and prosperous British protectorate.

bility for the conquest of most of the Sokoto empire. Thus, although the French eventually reached Lake Chad, they were kept to the southern edges of the Sahara, and most of the well-populated Hausa agricultural territory became the British protectorate of Northern Nigeria. In 1914 this was merged with the Yoruba territories, which had been entered from Lagos during the 1890s, and with the protectorate over the Niger delta region to constitute a single Colony and Protectorate of Nigeria.

ESTABLISHING TERRITORIAL BOUNDARIES

As early as 1898 Europeans had staked out colonies over all western Africa except for some 40,000 square miles of territory left to the Republic of Liberia. Portugal had taken virtually no active part in the scramble, and its once extensive influence was now confined within the 14,000 square miles that became the colony of Portuguese Guinea (today's Guinea-Bissau). Germany, the latecomer, had claimed the 33,000 square miles of Togo, together with the much larger Cameroon territory on the eastern borders of what is usually accepted as western Africa. France and Britain remained, as before, the main imperial powers.

France claimed by far the larger amount of territory, nearly 1.8 million square miles compared with some 450,000 square miles in the four enclaves secured by Britain. In other terms, however, France had done less well. Its territory included a large part of the Sahara, and the three inland colonies of French Sudan (modern Mali), Upper Volta (modern Burkina Faso), and Niger were by and large scantily populated and, because of their remoteness from the coast, were contributing little or nothing to the world economy. In 1897 the trade of the four British

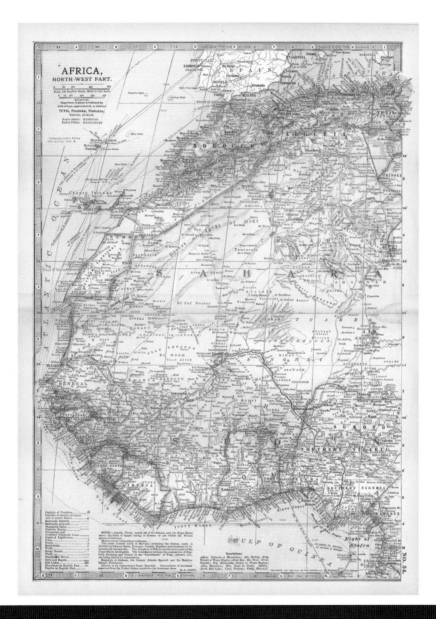

This map of northwestern Africa dates from around 1902. French possessions are orange, as is German Togoland. British possessions are pink. Independent Liberia and Portuguese Equatorial Guinea are green.

colonies was worth about $24 million, compared with about $14 million for the seven French territories, and their combined population of more than 20 million was more than twice as great.

The political boundaries established by the Europeans by 1898 (though usually not surveyed or demarcated on the ground until much later) largely determine the political map of western Africa today. The only subsequent change of significance followed the British and French conquests of the German colonies during World War I (1914–18). While the larger parts of both Togo and Cameroon were entrusted by the League of Nations to the French to administer as separate colonies, in each case a smaller western part was entrusted to Britain to be administered together with the Gold Coast and Nigeria respectively. Ultimately British Togo chose to join with the Gold Coast and so became part of the new independent Ghana. The northern part of British Cameroon similarly joined with Nigeria, but the southern part chose instead to federate with the former French Cameroon.

PROBLEMS OF MILITARY CONTROL

If 20 years had sufficed for the European powers to partition western African lands, at least a further

20 years were needed to establish colonial regimes that were effective throughout all the vast territories claimed by Europe and that were accepted by all the Africans involved. The first problem was a military one.

Small and mobile columns of African soldiers, led and trained by European officers and noncommissioned officers and equipped with precision rifles, machine guns, and artillery, rarely experienced much difficulty in defeating the great empires created by the 19th-century jihadists. These chose to meet the invaders in pitched battles in which their massed feudal levies, with few modern weapons and limited skill in their use, served only as targets for the superior firepower and discipline of their opponents. Once these battles had been lost, the surviving leaders were usually ready to acknowledge the Europeans as new overlords. The main problems were really ones of distance and logistics. Thus it was not until 1900–03 that Sir Frederick Lugard's forces were sufficiently established in northern Nigeria to defeat the Sokoto Fulani, while the French "pacification" of the even more remote territory further north, which eventually became their colony of Niger, was not really completed until the 1920s.

A much more serious military problem was often presented by smaller political units, which were ethnically more homogeneous and often more densely populated than the jihad empires. Their subjugation was often a protracted business in which the Europeans had to fight virtually for each settlement. This was the case with the British campaign against Asante in 1900–01, with the subjugation of the Sierra Leone protectorate in 1898–99, and above all, perhaps, with the advance of British power into the densely populated Igbo and Tiv territories, which was hardly complete until as late as 1918. Similarly, the most formidable resistance faced by the French came not from the Tukolor, but from the more southerly empire established from the 1860s onward from the hinterland of Sierra Leone to western Gonja by the Mande leader Samory Touré. Though Samory was a Muslim whose activities did much to consolidate the hold of Islam in his territories, he was not a cleric like Usman dan Fodio or al-Ḥājj ʿUmar. He came from a family of Dyula traders and soldiers, and the principles of his government recalled those of ancient Mali rather than of the jihad empires. Samory established his network of military and political control over territories long subject to Mande commercial penetration and settlement, and a number of campaigns had to be fought against him until he was finally captured and exiled by the French in 1898.

The Muslim reformer and military leader Samory Touré founded a powerful kingdom in West Africa and resisted French colonial expansion in the late 19th century.

Once the superior firepower and organization of the Europeans had secured their military supremacy, they were faced with an even larger problem; namely, how the small forces they commanded were to maintain a permanent occupation and effective control over the vast territories they had overrun. Lugard, for instance, had conquered the Sokoto empire with only about 3,000 soldiers, only 150 of whom were Europeans, and to administer his northern Nigerian colony of some 250,000 square miles and 10 million people he had a civil establishment of only 200 Europeans. This kind of situation persisted almost throughout the colonial period. At the end of the 1930s, for example, the European establishment available to the British governor of the Gold Coast to control nearly four million people was only 842. It is obvious, then, that the conquerors were often very slow to extend effective rule throughout their empires, and particularly to those parts of them that were most remote, presented serious political problems, or seemed least profitable.

INITIAL DIFFICULTY OF EUROPEAN ADMINISTRATION

No European control could be exercised without the cooperation of large numbers of Africans. This was secured in two ways. First, just as the Europeans had relied on Africans for the rank and file of their armies and police, so their administrations and economic enterprises could not function without a host of Africans employed as clerks, messengers, craftsmen of all kinds, and labourers. All of this employment offered new opportunities to Africans, and to ensure an efficient labour force all European administrations began to supplement and develop the schools begun by the missionaries.

As well as recruiting and training large numbers of Africans as auxiliaries in all spheres of European activity, the colonial powers also came to rely on African chiefs as essential intermediaries in the chain of authority between the colonial governments and their subjects at large. Both the French and the British colonial regimes were essentially hierarchical. The administration of each colony was entrusted to a governor who was responsible to a colonial minister in the government in Europe (in the French case, via a governor-general at Dakar). These governors were assisted by senior officials and a secretariat in the colonial capital, and their decisions and orders were transmitted for implementation to provincial and district commissioners. A district officer, however, could not deal directly with each of the tens, or even hundreds, of thousands of Africans in his care. He therefore gave orders either to the traditional chiefs or to Africans who had been recognized as local rulers by his government, and these intermediaries passed them on to the people at large.

In this connection a difference of theory began to be discernible between French and British policy. The French regarded the local African chiefs as the lowest elements in a single administrative machine. This administration was to be conducted on entirely French lines. The British, on the other hand, came to believe more and more in "indirect rule." British authority was not to reach directly down to each individual African subject. While the British retained overall control of a colony's administration, it was to be made effective at the district level by cultivating and by molding the governments of the traditional African rulers.

Indirect rule was neither a new nor a specifically British expedient. Maclean had been an indirect ruler on the Gold Coast in the 1830s; Goldie had proposed indirect rule for the empire his Royal Niger Company had hoped to conquer; and, in the early days of their expansion, the French had often had no alternative but to seek to control their newly won territories through the agency of the African governments they had conquered. Once they were firmly established, however, the French almost invariably moved away from the practice. The British, on the other hand, evolved a theory of indirect rule that they tried to apply systematically to their colonies during the first half of the 20th century. This was largely due to the influence of Lugard. In 1900–06 he had seen no other way to control the vast population in northern Nigeria, whose rulers he had defeated, and he had subsequently been made governor-general (1912–19) of a united Nigeria, which was by far the most important

F.D. Lugard played a major part in Britain's colonial history, serving in East Africa, West Africa, and Hong Kong.

British colony in Africa. After his retirement to Britain, he became a dominating influence on the formation of colonial administrative policy, so that indirect rule became accepted as the ideal philosophy of government for British tropical Africa.

Not all areas of western Africa were as suitable for Lugardian indirect rule as northern Nigeria.

Lugard himself experienced considerable problems in trying to apply it to the largely chiefless societies of eastern Nigeria and to the Yoruba of the southwest, where authority and law were not as clear-cut. In the Gold Coast indirect rule proved more acceptable to the Asante than the direct rule imposed after the conquest of 1900–01. Farther south, however, the Western-style economy and modes of thought had made such inroads that there were endless problems in the implementation of indirect rule, and the full constitutional apparatus for it was hardly installed until the 1940s.

The development of indirect rule also implied a contradiction with an earlier tradition of British colonial government, that of the colonial legislative council. The governors of British colonies were allowed more initiative than French governors and were supposed to exercise this in the interests of their individual territories insofar as these did not contradict the overriding British interest. To help them in this, each colony was equipped with a legislative council that included representatives of local opinion, and this council's consent was normally required before laws were enacted or the colonial government's budget was approved.

The institution of the legislative council had evolved from experience with settler colonies outside

Africa; when such councils were introduced into tropical Africa from the 1840s onward, most of their members were colonial officials. A minority of "unofficial" members represented trade and the professions rather than the traditional communities, and these were not elected but were nominated by the governor. However, 19th-century colonial officials, traders, and professionals were almost as likely to be black as white, and the early legislative councils were by no means ineffective vehicles for the expression of African interests and of criticisms of British policy. It was thus possible both for the British and for the educated African elite in their colonies to view the legislative councils as embryo parliaments that would eventually become composed of elected African members who would control the executive governments, which would themselves, through the growth of education in the colonies, become more and more composed of African officials.

Although very little thought was given to the matter, because it was supposed that the development might take centuries, it was supposed that the British colonies in Africa would follow the example of Canada and Australia and ultimately emerge as self-governing members of the empire. The remote future for the French colonies, on the other hand, was thought to be the acculturation (*assimilation*) of their people, so that ultimately they would all become full French citizens, the colonies would be integrated with metropolitan France, and the African citizens would share equally with the French-born in its institutions.

Both of these ideals were more appropriate to the colonial situations in western Africa before the great scramble for territory that began in 1879, when the colonies were comparatively small territories in which European influence had been slowly but steadily gaining ground for a considerable period. They were effectively shelved when it came to grappling with the problem of governing the enormously greater numbers of Africans without any real previous contacts with European ways who were quickly brought under colonial rule in the years after 1879. Thus, on the French side, though those born in the four major communes (Saint-Louis, Gorée, Rufisque, and Dakar) of the old colony of Senegal continued to enjoy the French citizenship that they had been granted prior to 1879, other Africans became French subjects (possessing the obligations of citizens but not their rights), who could only qualify for citizenship after stringent tests. By 1937, out of an estimated 15 million people under French rule in western Africa, only some 80,500 were citizens, and only 2,500 of these had acquired their citizenship by means other than the accident of birth in one of the four communes.

In the British colonies, however, where the legislative councils were already a reality, there was a dichotomy between them and the institution of indirect rule. Initially, insofar as this was resolved at all, it was at the expense of the development of the legislative councils. Thus the competence of the council in the Gold Coast was not extended to Asante before 1946, while in Nigeria until 1922 the council's competence was restricted to the small territory of Lagos. It was not until 1922 that any elected members appeared in the councils, and they remained for a generation a small proportion of the total unofficial membership, chosen only by tiny electorates in a few coastal towns. For the rest, the African population remained firmly under British control through the mechanism of indirect rule. The implication was not only that the norms of African society and political behaviour were far removed from those of western Europe but also that the British had by no means accepted that African society and politics would or should evolve in that direction. Those few Africans who had become educated and acculturated in Western ways were not thought to be representative of the mass. There was a move to exclude local Africans from the colonial administration, which became regarded as a professional service, liable to serve anywhere in Africa, with the role of holding the ring until, in some unexplained fashion, the native administrations under indirect rule had developed sufficiently to make British control superfluous.

COLONIAL RULE

In fact, of course, the very existence of colonial rule meant that the fabric of African societies was exposed to alien forces of change of an intensity and on a scale unparalleled in the previous history of western Africa. Hitherto remote territories like Niger and Mauritania, where there had been very little change since the introduction of Islam, were from about 1900 suddenly caught up in the same tide of aggressive material changes that had for some time been affecting the coastal societies in Senegal or in the southern Gold Coast and Nigeria. From the African point of view, there was little to choose between the European colonial powers. Portugal, despite the fact that it was virtually bankrupt at the onset of the colonial period, was as significant a bringer of change as France, Germany, and Britain. In fact, in the long run, a strange combination of its poverty with memories of its older colonial tradition were to make Portugal's sense of

LIBERIA

Liberia's formal status as an independent republic did not mean that the forces of change associated with the colonial period were excluded from
its territory. Its African American ruling elite were
orphaned members of a very rapidly changing
Western society, who felt it essential to impose
its ethos on black Africa. While colonial administrators often had a narrow, 19th-century concept
of government as an arbiter, rather than as an
active protagonist of change, the Liberians felt
a need actively to enlist the support of Western
capital and enterprise if they were to consolidate
their rule over African peoples and to maintain
the independence of their republic.

Up to 1912 the inexperience and relative
weakness of Liberia's ruling elite meant that
it achieved little except to run up a dangerous
indebtedness to ingenuous and potentially rapa-
cious European investors. In 1925–26, however,
the tide began to turn for them when the American Firestone Tire & Rubber Company, worried

(CONTINUED ON THE NEXT PAGE)

(CONTINUED FROM THE PREVIOUS PAGE)

lest its supplies of raw material should become a British colonial monopoly, secured a new American loan for Liberia and began to operate a one-million-acre plantation concession in the hinterland of Monrovia. The country was now supplied with a sure access to world trade, and its government with the means to achieve a stable revenue. Within 25 years Liberia's foreign trade grew from less than $3 million a year to some $45 million, and government revenue from a mere $500,000 a year to nearly $10 million. The evident dangers that Liberia might become too dependent on a single export crop, and that it and its administration might become sole fiefs of the American company, began to disappear when during World War II U.S. strategic interests caused its government to begin to give aid to Liberia and to develop its first modern port, and when in the 1950s both American and European interests began to exploit Liberia's large-scale deposits of high-grade iron ore. By the 1960s Liberia was on the way to becoming one of the richer western African countries, and the ruling elite began to feel sufficiently secure to share both some of its political power and some of its prosperity with the native peoples.

a *mission civilisatrice* even more pervasive than that of its stronger rivals.

A cardinal rule for all colonial administrations in Africa before the 1930s was that colonies ought not to be a financial burden on the metropolitan governments and their taxpayers: the cost of colonial administration and development should be covered by the local revenues they could raise. So long as such a doctrine was maintained, it was impossible for any but the richest colonial administrations to devise coherent plans for the economic development of their territories; indeed, prior to the 1940s, the colonial government of the Gold Coast was virtually unique in putting forward such a plan, and then only in the 1920s, which were by and large exceptionally prosperous years.

The principal sources of revenue were (1) duties on the trade entering and leaving the territory and (2) direct taxation (usually a poll tax or hut tax). But only those coastal colonies that had already entered the world economy prior to about 1880 had much in the way of trade on which customs duties might be levied or a sufficient internal production of commodities and circulation of money to produce any significant income from direct taxation. Other territories—such as British northern Nigeria, or the French colonies of the Sudan (Mali) and Niger—

could not really provide enough revenue to support
even the most essential administrative services, such
as policing or—for that matter—tax gathering. For
some time, therefore, these administrations were in
receipt of grants-in-aid from some central source,
and it was an attempt to shift this burden from metropolitan resources that as much as anything led the
French in 1895 to bring together their western African
colonies under a government general and that led
Lugard to argue for the unification of the Nigerian
colonies, which he eventually achieved in 1912–14.
In each case it seemed advisable to use some of the
comparatively buoyant revenues of the coastal
territories to subsidize the administrations of those in
the interior.

It was obvious enough that what was needed was
to increase the European commercial penetration of
western Africa. But only the prospect of the most
lucrative prizes could induce private European
investors to place substantial amounts of capital in
Africa in advance of adequate European administrations that could guarantee the safety and security of
their investments and in advance of the economic
infrastructures that would ensure their efficient
deployment. The only lure that really operated to
attract European investment in advance of the
provision of such services was the prospect of rich

mineral deposits. The greater part of western Africa's mineral wealth lies in ores such as those of iron, aluminum, and manganese, which are extremely bulky in relation to their value and require very large investments in transport and other facilities before they can be economically worked, and for which there was relatively little overseas demand before the 1930s. The possibilities of diamond mining in Sierra Leone and the Gold Coast were not really recognized until the 1930s. In effect then, it was only the gold of the Gold Coast and Asante forests and, to a lesser extent, the tin of the Bauchi plateau in central Nigeria, that attracted the early attention of European investors.

Modern methods of gold mining first began to be employed on the Gold Coast as early as 1878, but the industry could not make much headway before 1902. By that time the colonial government had taken the decisive steps of defeating Asante, beginning to build a railway system, and establishing an effective civil administration in the relevant areas, which could ensure proper land surveys and some means of controlling and adjudicating disputes over the ownership of land and the validity of concessions of it. Bauchi tin mining began much later, in 1903, but similar, if less acute, difficulties prevented much progress before 1914.

Despite their poverty, and despite the risk of saddling the home governments and taxpayers with unwanted expenditure, colonial governments found that there was no alternative to their providing the basic infrastructures needed by the vast territories they claimed to rule. It was impossible to wait for private European enterprise to provide railways, harbours, telegraph lines, roads, medical services, schools, and all the other things that were needed to support an effective government, let alone to provide some possibility of economic growth sufficient to pay for better government.

FRENCH TERRITORIES

The problems facing the French were much more formidable than those facing the British. The British colonies were essentially based on territories close to the sea, in which European trade had been long established and whose African peoples were already accustomed to producing for the world market. The French had such a colony in Senegal, but from this they had expanded over vast, remote, and thinly populated territories that required very considerable investment before they could be efficiently adminis-tered or developed. By and large the French public had appreciably less capital to invest overseas than the British public had. By 1936 it was estimated that, whereas the British colonies in western Africa had attracted about $560 million of capital, the total outside investment in French West Africa amounted only to some $155 million.

French strategy was initially to open up and develop its western African empire from a base in Senegal on the same Sénégal–Niger river axis along which it had been conquered. As early as 1882 work was begun on a railway to link the heads of navigation of the two rivers at Kayes and at Bamako (which became the capital of the French Sudan). But this line was not completed until 1906, by which time it had become evident that Saint-Louis, at the mouth of the Sénégal River, was not capable of development into a modern port, and that the Sénégal was really suitable for navigation for only three months in the year. So first a railway was completed from Saint-Louis to the new harbour of Dakar in the lee of Cape Verde (1885), and then during 1907–24 a line was built directly from Dakar (since 1902 the federal capital for French West Africa) to Kayes to bypass the Sénégal River altogether.

The construction of an effective west-east transport system from the coast to the upper Niger thus took some 42 years to complete, and the only part of it that was profitable was that serving the peanut-growing areas of Senegal. There was a lag of some 20 years after 1924 before the thinly populated and impoverished French Sudan could respond to the stimulus of its improved communications with the outside world. Indeed the only major crop developed for the world market that could withstand the high costs of transport to the coast—over some 700 miles of railway—was cotton, and that only after considerable further investment in irrigation. Ultimately the main economic role of the Sudan was to provide foodstuffs for Senegal, whose peasant farmers found it more profitable to concentrate on growing peanuts for export.

By 1914 French economic strategy had shifted from the concept of opening up the inland territories of the French Sudan, Upper Volta, and Niger, to the encouragement of agricultural production in the coastal colonies. To a limited extent, the way was pioneered by European plantations, more especially perhaps in the Ivory Coast. Generally these colonies were made remunerative by administrative pressures to induce African farmers to produce for export. Ultimately, just as the economy of Senegal had become largely dependent on the export of peanuts, so that of French Guinea became dependent on bananas (though at the very end of the colonial period, European and American capital began the successful exploitation of considerable deposits of bauxite and iron ore), and the economies of Dahomey and of Togo (after its conquest from Germany) became dependent on palm produce. The most dramatic successes were achieved in the Ivory Coast, where considerable exports were developed of coffee, cocoa, bananas, and lumber. Railways were built from suitable points on the coast to facilitate the export of these crops.

In the 45 years from 1912–13 to 1956–57, the French had boosted the foreign trade of their western African empire from about $58 million a year to about $600 million a year, with the result that the revenues available to their colonial administrations increased from about $8.5 million a year to as much as $315 million. (These figures exclude the part of Togo that was incorporated in the French empire only after 1914–18, and the trade and revenue of which by the mid-1950s were worth some $24 million and $4 million a year respectively.) In absolute terms in relation to the total population, which in the same period is thought to have doubled to an estimated 19 million, the results were not so spectacular; in 1956–57 foreign trade per capita overall amounted to about $32 and government revenue to about $17. The significance of the figures is also obscured by the federal system to which all the colonies except

Togo were subject and which was deliberately used to enable the richer colonies to help the poorer. The trade and revenue figures cannot be easily broken down between the individual colonies. Whereas the estimated gross national products (GNPs) for Senegal and the Ivory Coast were in the order of $180 and $160 per capita respectively (the former considerably inflated by the colony's possession of the federal capital), only Togo (about $73) and French Guinea and Sudan (about $58 and $53, respectively) were thought to have GNPs per capita higher than $40.

BRITISH TERRITORIES

Each of the four British colonies must necessarily be treated as an independent unit, as each was so treated in British policy. The Gambia was merely a strip of land, averaging only seven miles in width, on either side of 292 miles of navigable waterway penetrating into what otherwise was French Senegal. Even in the 1950s its population did not exceed 300,000, and the possibilities for any sort of development were limited. In fact the colony achieved a fair degree of prosperity by concentrating on the production of peanuts, grown in part by farmers who migrated annually from Senegal for the purpose. By 1956–57

foreign trade was some $60 per capita and govern-
ment revenue $14.

The Sierra Leone situation was one of a relatively
dense population exploiting or even overexploiting
a poor environment for its subsistence, and initially
the most that was achieved was to develop some
palm produce for export. During the 1930s the situation began to change when European companies
began to exploit extensive diamond-bearing gravels
and to mine high-grade iron ore. By the mid-1950s
foreign trade, which had been $14 million ($9 per
capita) in 1913–14, had risen to $101 million ($44).
About half of this was based on the activities of the
foreign-owned mining companies. These provided
little local employment; and furthermore, large
numbers of people had been led to abandon farming to dig for diamonds on their own account. This
gave rise to numerous social, economic, and political problems, because legally the diamond-bearing
grounds had been conceded to the European companies. These factors may explain why the increase
in government revenue, and hence the capacity of
the government to sponsor further development, was
low in comparison with other western African territories. It rose from $3.6 million ($2.40 per capita) in
1913–14 to $27 million ($11.70) in 1956–57, a factor
of increase of 4.9, which compares unfavourably with

a factor of 21.1 for French West Africa as a whole, 11.4 for the Gold Coast, 6.1 for Nigeria, or even 5.9 for the Gambia.

The Gold Coast was a complete contrast, indeed one of the most successful examples of colonial development anywhere in British tropical Africa. The people of its coastlands were long accustomed to world trade, and indeed to British rule, with the result that the Gold Coast entered the colonial period with a very high level of economic activity. In 1912–13 its foreign trade was worth $42.5 million ($28.30 per capita) while government revenue was $6.5 million ($4.30 per capita). Subsequent development was facilitated by the possession, within a manageable area that was adequately but not too densely populated, of a considerable variety of resources.

The first railway was built inland from Sekondi in the southeastern Gold Coast between 1898 and 1903 with the dual purpose of supporting gold mining and ensuring political control of Asante. This railway subsequently was used for the removal of manganese ore and bauxite. Extensive diamond diggings, worked equally by individual Africans and by European companies, began to be developed from 1919 onward. But the mainstay of the economy became cocoa, which local farmers began to produce on small plots in the forest toward the end of the

19th century. They found a reliable market for their produce. Cocoa became the most valuable export when it outranked gold in 1913, and thereafter went on to contribute more than four-fifths of exports and to constitute something between a third and a half of the world's supply.

The prosperity derived from cocoa in the 1920s enabled the governor, Sir Frederick Gordon Guggisberg, to pledge the country's revenues for loans to finance a coherent program of economic and social development. The Gold Coast's first deep-water port was built at Takoradi, the cocoa-producing forestlands were equipped with a comprehensive railway and road system, and the foundations were laid for educational and medical services as good as any in tropical Africa. Subsequent development was severely checked by the Great Depression of the 1930s and by events of World War II, but by the mid-1950s the postwar demand for tropical produce generated trade for the Gold Coast, estimated to have fewer than five million people, of about $500 million a year, not far short of that generated by all the 19 million people living in French West Africa. Government revenue reached the high level of $27.50 per person, by far the highest in western Africa, while the GNP of about $200 per person was probably higher than that of any tropical African country.

Nigeria provides yet another contrast. The people of its southern territories, like those of the southern Gold Coast or of Senegal, had long been in touch with the world economy. In 1912–13 the country's trade, at some $65 million a year, was 50 percent higher than the Gold Coast's and greater even than the combined total for the eight French colonies, including Senegal. But Nigeria was a giant territory, three times as large as the other three British colonies put together, and though compared with the French federation it was relatively small and compact (373,000 square miles), it had the same problem of extending over a considerable area of the remote western Sudan. This could not be ignored—as the much smaller northern Gold Coast or such northern French colonies as Niger were effectively ignored—because the Nigerian Sudan contained more than half the country's enormous population. By the mid-1950s the Nigerian population was more than 32 million, more than half that of western Africa.

Two things were clearly needed: first, to develop a transport system to make it possible to control and open up the populous north; and, second, to use some of the wealth generated from the growth of foreign trade in the south to stimulate development in the north. No coherent policy was possible, however, before the amalgamation of the separate colonial administrations, which was achieved under Lugard in 1912–14. Initially, even railway building tended to provoke disunion. The first line was built inland from Lagos in 1898–1901 to open up Yorubaland. Before this line was extended to the north across the Niger, the northern government had begun its own railway, from the highest point of navigation on the river, through its new administrative capital of Kaduna, to Kano. In 1912 this was intercepted by an extension of the Lagos line, and subsequently branches were built to areas active in tin mining and the cultivation of peanuts. Finally, another line was built from a new eastern port, Port Harcourt, to the coal mines around Enugu (1916), and this was subsequently extended to Kaduna (1927). By the 1930s Nigeria had 1,900 miles of railway, nearly as many as those possessed by all the French territories together (2,160 miles) but built at nearly twice the cost.

While southern Nigerian development, based essentially on cocoa production in the west and processing of palm oil and kernels in the east, followed much the same pattern as that of the southern Gold Coast, and with essentially similar social consequences, the development of peanuts as the prime export crop of the north did not produce comparable results for its appreciably larger population. By the mid-1950s the trade of Nigeria, at some $800 million a year, was still greater than that of all French West Africa in total, but it was appreciably less per capita, $25.30 compared with $32.20, and the annual revenue available to government, at $173 million, was small in proportion to the total population, only about $5.50 per capita. Inevitably a serious gap had developed between the economic and social progress of the south and that of the north.

DECOLONIZATION AND THE REGAINING OF INDEPENDENCE

The end of the colonial period and the establishment during 1957–76 of all the former colonies as independent states was attributable both to a change in European attitudes toward Africa and the possession of colonies and to an African reaction to colonial rule born of the economic and social changes it had produced.

Europeans had colonized western Africa in the later 19th and early 20th centuries confident that their civilization was immensely superior to anything Africa had produced or could produce. Yet hardly had their colonies been established than these convictions began to be challenged. World War I, and the immense misery and loss of life it caused, led some Europeans to doubt whether nations who could so brutally mismanage their own affairs had any moral right to dictate to other peoples. Some reflection of this view was seen in the League of Nations and the system of mandates applied to the former German colonies. Although in western Africa these were entrusted to either French or British administration, the mandated territories did not become the absolute possessions of the conquerors, and the role of the new rulers was declared to be to equip the mandated territories and their peoples for self-government.

A second shock to European self-confidence came with the Great Depression of the 1930s, when trade and production shrank and millions of Europeans had no work. It began to be argued that a remedy lay in more active development of the overseas territories controlled by Europe. If more European capital and skills were directed to the colonies, so that they could produce more raw materials for European industry more efficiently, both Europe and the colonies would gain; as the colonies became wealthier through the exploitation of their resources, the people of the colonies would buy more from Europe.

In 1929 Britain had enacted the first Colonial Development Act, providing that small amounts of

British government money could be used for colonial economic development, thus breaking the deadlock by which the only colonial governments that could embark on development programs to increase the wealth of their subjects, and to improve their own revenues, were those that already commanded sufficient revenue to pay for the programs or to service the loans the programs required. The idea that the colonies should be actively developed, in the European as much as in the African interest, was broadened during and after World War II. Transport and currency problems made it urgent for Britain and France to exploit strategic raw materials in their colonies. Furthermore, during 1940–44, when France itself was in German hands, it was only from the colonies and with their resources that Gen. Charles de Gaulle and his associates could continue the fight.

The British funding policy, initiated in 1929, of providing the funds needed for colonial development was greatly expanded in the 1940s and extended to social as well as economic plans. After the war the governments of both Britain and France required their colonial administrations to draw up comprehensive development plans and in effect offered to provide the funds for those that could not be funded from local resources.

In view of past history, the need for such plans was probably greater in the French colonies than in the British, and the French West African program for 1946–55 envisaged the investment of $1,108,000,000, compared with programs totaling $549 million for the four British colonies. Virtually all of the financing for the French program came from France itself. But some of the British colonies had built up considerable reserves from the high prices commanded by their produce during the war and immediate postwar years, and they themselves were able to provide much of the money needed. This tended to accentuate already existing disparities. In the extreme case the Gold Coast plan envisaged spending $300 million, only 4 percent of which was British money. This was the same level of expenditure, roughly $60 per capita, as envisaged for French West Africa. Nigeria's program, with a contribution from Britain of 42 percent, proposed to spend $220 million—only about $7 per capita. The figures for Sierra Leone were $21 million, 45 percent from the United Kingdom, and $10 per capita; and for the tiny Gambia $8 million, 35 percent, and $27 per capita.

The accompanying political changes were more cautious and turned out to be inadequate to accommodate African aspirations—which had been derived from social changes occasioned during the classical period of colonial rule and further whetted by the policies of active economic development. On the British side, during 1945–48 the legislative councils were reformed so that African representatives outnumbered the European officials. Many of these African members, however, were still government nominees, and, because of the British attachment to indirect rule, those who were elected were mainly representative of the traditional chiefs.

Political advance for the French colonies was naturally seen in terms of increased African participation in French political life. In 1944 it was proposed that the colonies become overseas territories of France. Delegates from the colonies in fact participated in the making of the new postwar French constitution, but this was subject to referenda in which metropolitan French votes predominated. The constitution eventually adopted in 1946 was less liberal to Africans than they had been led to expect.

THE EMERGENCE OF AFRICAN LEADERS

By the later 1940s, however, there were appreciable numbers of Africans in both the French and the British colonies who had emerged from traditional society through the new opportunities for economic advancement and education. In coastal areas Christian missionaries and their schools had advanced with the European administrations. The colonial governments, requiring African subordinates for their system, commonly aided and developed the elementary and vocational education initiated by the Christian missions and often themselves provided some sort of higher education for the chiefly classes whose cooperation they required. If rather little of this education had penetrated to the Sudan by the 1940s, in some coastal areas Africans had become eager to invest some of their increasing wealth in education, which was seen as the key to European strength.

Relatively few Africans started up the French educational ladder—school attendance by the mid-1950s was some 340,000, about 1.7 percent of the total population—but those who did found themselves in a system identical with that in France. In British West Africa schools had got a footing before there was much administration to control them, and their subsequent development was more independent. The British educational system therefore developed into a pyramid with a much broader base than the French one. By the mid-1950s there were more than two million schoolchildren in Nigeria, about 6 percent of the total population and a much higher proportion of the population of the south, in which the schools were concentrated; in the Gold Coast there were nearly 600,000, some 12 percent of the population. Many more people in the British than in the French territories thus got some education, and appreciably more were able to attend universities. In 1948 universities were established in the Gold Coast and Nigeria; by 1960 the former territory had about 4,500 university graduates and the latter more than 5,000. The first French African university was a federal institution at Dakar opened in 1950; by 1960 the total number of graduates in French West Africa was about 1,800.

By the 1940s there was enough education to make European-style political activity possible in all the coastal colonies. Such activity may be traced back to at least the 1890s, when Gold Coast professionals and some chiefs founded the Aborigines' Rights Protection Society (ARPS) to prevent the wholesale expropriation of African lands by European entrepreneurs or officials. The ARPS went on to campaign against the exclusion of qualified Africans from the colonial administration. Following this, in 1918–20, a National Congress of British West Africa was formed by professionals to press for the development of the legislative councils in all the British colonies into elective assemblies controlling the colonial administrations.

In French West Africa early political activity was concentrated in the four towns of Senegal whose people possessed political rights before 1946. Because the seat of power was very clearly in France, with Senegalese electors sending a deputy to the French National Assembly, the result by the 1930s was the emergence of a Senegalese Socialist party allied to the Socialists in France.

By the late 1940s both the French and the British territories possessed an educated, politicized class, which felt frustrated in its legitimate expectations; it had made no appreciable progress in securing any real participation in the system of political control. In fact, anything approaching effective African participation seemed more remote than ever. Implementation of the development programs led to a noticeable increase in the number of Europeans employed by the colonial regimes and their associated economic enterprises. On the other hand, because many Africans had served with, and received educational and technical training with, the British and French armies, the war had led to a great widening of both African experience and skills. Furthermore, the postwar economic situation was one in which African farmers were receiving high prices for their produce but could find little to spend their money on, and in which the eagerly awaited development plans were slow to mature because European capital goods were in short supply.

THE FORMATION OF AFRICAN INDEPENDENCE MOVEMENTS

There thus developed a general feeling among the intelligentsia that the colonies were being deliberately exploited by ever more firmly entrenched European political and economic systems and that there had developed a new, wider, and mobilizable public to appeal to for support. In 1946 politicians in French West Africa organized a federation-wide political association, the African Democratic Rally (RDA). The RDA and its members in the French National Assembly aligned themselves with the French Communist Party, the only effective opposition to the governments of the Fourth Republic. The result, during 1948–50, was the virtual suppression of the RDA in Africa by the colonial administrations.

In British West Africa the tensions were greatest in the Gold Coast. In 1947 the established politicians brought in Kwame Nkrumah, who had studied in the United States and Britain and had been active in the Pan-African movement, to organize a nationalist party with mass support. In 1948 European trading houses were boycotted, and some rioting took place

in the larger towns. An official inquiry concluded
that the underlying problem was political frustration
and that African participation in government should
be increased until the colony became self-governing.
In 1951, therefore, a new constitution was introduced in which the legislative council gave way to
an assembly dominated by African elected members,
to which African ministers were responsible for the
conduct of much government business. By this time
Nkrumah had organized his own mass political party,

The Ghanaian nationalist leader Kwame Nkrumah led the Gold Coast's drive for independence from Britain and would later preside over its emergence as the new nation of Ghana.

able to win any general election, and during the following years he negotiated with the British a series of concessions that resulted in 1957 in the Gold Coast becoming the independent state of Ghana.

Once the British had accepted the principle of cooperating with nationalist politicians, their other western African colonies began to follow the example set by the Gold Coast. But Nkrumah had been greatly aided by the high price for cocoa in the 1950s (which meant that by 1960 Ghana's trade was worth $630 million a year and that government revenue, at more than $280 million, was broadly adequate to give the people what they wanted in the way of modernizing programs) and by the comparatively high level and generally wide spread of education in a sizable yet compact territory that was without too serious ethnic divisions. The other colonies were not so well placed.

The small size of The Gambia was the principal factor contributing to the delay of its independence until 1965. Sierra Leone was a densely populated country that was appreciably poorer than Ghana (its GNP per capita, at about $70, being approximately one-third of Ghana's) and in which there was a wide disparity in levels of education and wealth between the Creoles—the descendants of liberated slaves who lived in and around Freetown—and the rest of the people. When independence was achieved in 1961, these deeply rooted problems had been papered over rather than solved.

Nigeria presented the greatest challenge to British and African policymakers alike. In the south two nationalist parties emerged, the Action Group (AG), supported primarily by the Yoruba of the west, and the National Convention of Nigerian Citizens (NCNC), whose prime support came from the Igbo of the east. These parties expected the whole country quickly to follow the Ghanaian pattern of constitutional change. But any elective central assembly was bound to be dominated by the north, which had some 57 percent of the population and whose economic and social development had lagged far behind. The north's political leaders—most of whom were conservative Muslim aristocrats closely allied with the British through indirect rule—were not at all eager to see their traditional paramountcy invaded by aggressive and better-educated leaders from the south.

The first political expedient was to convert Nigeria into a federation of three regions. In 1957 this allowed the east and the west to achieve internal self-government without waiting for the north, but it left open the questions of how politics were to be conducted at the centre and how Nigerian independence was to be secured. At this juncture it occurred to the northern leaders that by allying themselves to one of the southern parties they might maintain their local monopoly of power and gain prestige in the country as a whole by asking for its independence. The problem of central politics was thus resolved when the northern leaders entered a coalition federal government with the NCNC, and in 1960 Nigeria became independent.

Meanwhile, in French West Africa the RDA, led by Félix Houphouët-Boigny, broke with the Communist Party. The votes of a small bloc of African deputies in the French National Assembly were of considerable value to the shifting coalitions of non-Communist parties that made up the unstable French governments of the 1950s, and the RDA began to seek to influence these governments to allow greater freedom to the colonies.

By 1956 Houphouët-Boigny's policy had secured a widening of the colonial franchises and the beginnings of a system by which each colony was on the way to becoming a separate unit in which African ministers would be responsible for some of the conduct of government. The implications of this approach, however, did not meet with the approval of some other African leaders, most notable among them Léopold Senghor in Senegal and Ahmed Sékou Touré in Guinea. Senghor had stood outside the RDA since the

Houphouët-Boigny was a doctor and the son of a wealthy Baule chief. He became the president of Côte d'Ivoire (Ivory Coast) when it won independence in 1960 and remained in power until his death in 1993.

LÉOPOLD SENGHOR

Most of the adult life of Léopold Senghor was spent in politics. As president of Senegal for 20 years, he proved to be an effective chief executive. Senghor was also noted as one of Africa's leading writers. He has been called the greatest African poet writing in a European language (French). His poems and political philosophy express his concept of negritude, a literary movement that he described as the "sum total of cultural values of the Negro-African world." His poetry collections include *Chants d'Ombre* (1945), *Nocturnes* (1961), and *Élégies majeures* (1979). Two prose works are *Nationhood and the African Road to Socialism* (1961) and *The Poetry of Action* (1980).

Léopold Sédar Senghor was born in Joal, Senegal (then part of French West Africa), on October 9, 1906. He attended a Roman Catholic mission school and a seminary before transferring to a lycée (college-preparatory high school) in Dakar. In 1928 he went to Paris on a scholarship and studied at the Lycée Louis-le-Grand and the Sorbonne. He taught school until 1939 when he was drafted into the French army to serve in World War II. In 1940 he was captured by the Germans. He spent two years in a prison camp. Upon his release he joined the French Resistance.

After the war Senghor was elected as a French National Assembly deputy from Senegal. In 1956 he became the mayor of Thiès, Senegal's railroad centre, and was reelected deputy. He founded the Senegalese Progressive Union (after 1976, the Socialist party). When Senegal became independent in August 1960, Senghor was elected president. He retired in 1980.

As chief executive, Senghor tried to modernize Senegal's agriculture, instill a sense of enlightened citizenship, combat corruption and inefficiency, forge closer ties with his African neighbors, and continue cooperation with the French. He advocated an African socialism based on African realities, free of both atheism and excessive materialism. He sought an open, democratic, humanistic socialism that shunned such slogans as "dictatorship of the proletariat." A vigorous spokesman for the Third World, he protested unfair terms of trade that worked to the disadvantage of the agricultural nations. In 1984 he became the first black inducted into the French Academy, the prestigious literary association. He died on December 20, 2001, in Verson, France.

days of its alliance with the Communists, which he had thought could only bring disaster. Together with Sékou, who had remained within the RDA, he argued that Houphouët-Boigny's policy would split up the western African federation into units that would be too small and poor to resist continued French domination.

In 1958 the French Fourth Republic collapsed and de Gaulle was returned to power. On September 28, 1958, in a referendum, the colonies were offered full internal self-government as fellow members with France of a French Community that would deal with supranational affairs. All of the colonies voted for this scheme except Guinea, where Sékou Touré led the people to vote for complete independence. Senegal and the French Sudan were then emboldened in 1959 to come together in a Federation of Mali and to ask for and to receive complete independence within the community. These two territories separated in the following year, but all the others now asked for independence before negotiating conditions for association with France, and by 1960 all the former French colonies were de jure independent states.

By that time only the excessively conservative regimes of Portugal and Spain sought to maintain the colonial principle in western Africa. Encouraged and aided by independent neighbours, Guinean nationalists took up arms in 1962 and after 10 years of fighting expelled the Portuguese from three-quarters of Portuguese Guinea. In 1974 the strain of this war and of wars in Mozambique and Angola caused the Portuguese people and army to overthrow their dictatorship. Independence was quickly recognized for Guinea-Bissau in 1974 and for the Cape Verde Islands and São Tomé and Príncipe in 1975.

In 1959 the status of Spanish Guinea was changed, and the region was reorganized into two provinces of overseas Spain, each of which was placed under a civil governor. The citizens, including the Africans, were granted the same rights as those enjoyed by the citizens of Spain. In 1963 a measure of economic and administrative autonomy for the two provinces—which were henceforth known as Equatorial Guinea—was agreed on by plebiscite. The movement toward independence began to take shape at the end of 1967. Early the following year the Spanish government suspended autonomous political control and, with the subsequent approval of the Organization of African Unity (OAU), proposed that a national referendum be held to approve the new constitution. The constitution was overwhelmingly approved on August 11 and was followed by parliamentary elections in September and by the proclamation of independence on October 12, 1968. However, within ten years, the nation was plunged into chaos.

CHAPTER THREE

CENTRAL AFRICA

• •

C entral Africa is the region of Africa that straddles the Equator and is drained largely by the Congo River system. It comprises, according to common definitions, the Republic of the Congo (Brazzaville), the Central African Republic, and the Democratic Republic of the Congo (Kinshasa). Chad and Gabon are also included, because like Congo (Brazzaville) and the Central African Republic, they were once part of French Equatorial Africa. Sudan and South Sudan are not reliably considered part of Central Africa, but are included here because they, along with Chad, comprise the eastern part of the Sudan (the vast tract of open savanna plains extending across Africa south of the Sahara and north of the equatorial rain forests). Rwanda and Burundi, although they are located east of the East African Rift System, which forms the eastern divide of the Congo basin, are also often considered part of the region because of their long administrative connections with the former Belgian Congo. The island republic of São Tomé and Príncipe, off the Atlantic coast of Gabon, is also included in the region.

In the north are the savannas of Chad, the Central African Republic, Sudan, and South Sudan, stretching to the Nile River, and in the south is the largely forested area of the Congo River basin. The Congo area, in the centre of the continent, is an extension of the wet forestlands of the Guinea Coast; it extends to the lacustrine area of eastern Africa. That region is the largest area of secondary tropical forest in the world—only South America has more primary (i.e., undisturbed by humans) tropical forests.

In the 15th century Central Africa came into regular contact with the non-African world for the first time. Hitherto all external contact had been indirect and slow. Language, technology, and precious objects had spread to affect peoples' lives, but no regular contact was maintained. The earliest European settlement in the area was on the island of São Tomé, which was uninhabited when it was discovered, about 1470, by Portuguese navigators. The Portuguese sent out settlers (including many convicts and Jewish children who had been separated from their parents and expelled from Portugal) and brought African slaves to the islands to grow sugar. The slave trade became the primary reason for contact between Central Africa and the Europeans in the centuries that followed. After the abolition of the slave trade, European interests focused on the exploitation of resources, such as ivory, which eventually gave way to full-scale colonization.

DEVELOPMENT OF THE SLAVE TRADE

In the 1470s a colony of Portuguese was settled on the offshore island of São Tomé. The Portuguese had been experimenting with colonial plantations for more than a century and already had settlements on Cape Verde and the Canary and Madeira islands. On São Tomé they established fields of sugarcane and built sugar mills. This prototype industry, which was later taken to Brazil and the Caribbean, became the richest branch of Europe's colonial enterprise and had a lasting impact on the history of the African mainland. Settlers were unable to build plantations unaided and so recruited local support. European immigrants—predominantly, if not exclusively, male—sought out African consorts from the adjacent communities and established Creole families of plantation owners and managers. They also bought mainland slaves to work the estates. São Tomé became the first bridgehead for the great Atlantic slave trade, which was to have a deep and scarring influence on most of Central Africa.

Central African slaves taken to the island slave market were sold to three destinations. The strongest were sold to the Akan miners of the Gold Coast in West Africa, where royal Portuguese agents were able to buy up to half a ton of gold a year in exchange for imported commodities and slave workers from other parts of the continent. A second category of Central African slave was shipped to Europe and used both for domestic service in the town and for farm labour on the sparsely peopled estates that Portuguese Christians had conquered from Portuguese Muslims in the late Middle Ages. The third class of slave was put to work locally on the island.

The second attempt to build a European colony in Central Africa occurred in the kingdom of Kongo surrounding the mouth of the Congo River. Portuguese traders exploited a division in the ruling class to gain a foothold at the court and the support of a royal claimant, who adopted Christianity and assumed the title of Afonso I. The Portuguese had hoped to find precious metals, as they had done in West Africa and were later to do in southeastern Africa, but the only source of profit they could realize was the buying of slaves for the São Tomé

SÃO TOMÉ

The fortunes of the São Tomé plantations fluctuated over the centuries. Sugar gave way to coffee as the mainstay, and coffee in turn was replaced by cocoa in the 19th century. In the 20th century the island was at the centre of a humanitarian furor over the continued use of slaves on the plantations. Cocoa manufacturers boycotted the island, and the planters tried to improve the working conditions of their employees. In the meantime, however, Central Africa's premier colony had been eclipsed by other European ventures on the mainland.

Cocoa production fell after World War I, and the islands became isolated and notorious for the brutality and corruption that reigned on the plantations belonging to absentee planters and corporations. Attempts to force the local Forros to work on the plantations led to the Batepá Massacre in 1953, an event later often cited by São Toméans in their demands for independence as an example of the violence under Portuguese rule. The Committee for the Liberation of São Tomé and Príncipe was set up in exile in 1960; it changed its name to the Movement for the Liberation of São Tomé and Príncipe (MLSTP) in 1972. However, it consisted of only a small group of exiles, who were unable to mount a guerrilla challenge to the Portuguese on the islands.

The government that took power in Portugal after a coup in 1974 agreed to hand over power to the MLSTP in 1975, and virtually all Portuguese colonists fled to Portugal, fearing an independent black and communist government. Independence was granted on July 12, 1975.

market. The king was under increasing pressure to use his army to raid his neighbors for captives. Even the Roman Catholic priests attached to the colonial mission found that they had to finance their activities by trading in slaves. The increasing profitability of slaving, and the lack of alternative sources of exportable wealth, placed growing pressures on the kingdom. Eventually, after the death of Afonso, popular rebellion broke out on a virulent scale. In order to preserve their foothold, the Portuguese equipped the governor of São Tomé with an army of 600 musketeers with which to reconquer their mainland base and install a pliant king in the Kongo capital. The Latin American tradition of the Iberian conquistador was thus introduced into Central Africa.

The great slaving campaigns of the conquistadores began in the 1570s after the Kongo wars had been quelled. The Portuguese harbour of Luanda was taken over by the Spanish Habsburgs in 1580, when the two crowns were united, and a series of armed assaults were launched on the states of the Mbundu peoples of the interior. The basis of the invasion was the rising demand for slaves to colonize the huge but sparsely peopled provinces of Brazil. Many slaves were captured directly or obtained as ransom for important chiefs. Many more were obtained from long-distance trade networks that penetrated ever deeper into the heart of Central Africa both by river and by footpath. The primary imports of the traders were textiles from India, England, North Africa, or Portugal itself. But Portugal, even with the backing of Spain, was not economically strong enough to maintain its monopoly over the foreign trade in Central Africa. By the end of the 16th century, competitors were frequenting the coast.

The Dutch were the second colonial power to influence the history of Central Africa. Their impact was felt in ways rather different from that of the

Portuguese. They were more interested in commodities than in slaves and so opened up the market for ivory. The old hunting skills gained a new value as the market for tusks blossomed and commercial entrepreneurs organized caravans over long distances. Even the Twa forest dwellers were able to benefit from the hunting of elephants. By the mid-17th century, however, the Dutch had established their own American colonies and so joined in the scramble for slaves. They began to sell guns to their trading partners to facilitate the destruction of old communities and the capture of fugitives. The supply and sale of powder, lead, and muskets became profitable to the coastal brokers but devastating to the inland victims.

The geographic scale of the Central African slave trade was enormous. By the 18th century the supply routes to the Atlantic reached the middle of the continent and had begun to intersect with the long-distance trade to the Indian Ocean. As the trade spread, so did the search for political systems that could manage the traffic. The largest and most successful of the new merchant empires was the empire of the Lunda at the heart of the southern savanna. The Lunda people seem to have become aware of the slave trade as early as the 16th century. Wandering Lunda hunters and salt prospectors, known as Imbangala (or Jaga), entered Angola and recruited local followers into heavily armed bands that raided the countryside, sold their captives to European sailors, and eventually formed an alliance with the Portuguese conquistadores, who allowed them to set up their own kingdom in the Kasanje plain on the borders between Lunda and the European coastal enclaves. At first the kingdom of Kasanje acted solely as merchant brokers to the Portuguese, but, with the rise of rival European buyers on the northern Congo coast, its network spread farther afield. As the market expanded, so did the sources of supply. In the Lunda hinterland a powerful ruler adopting the title of Mwata Yamvo became chief supplier to the Kasanje intermediaries. The Lunda empire spread its commercial network not only to the west but also eastward until it had outlets to the lower Zambezi River and the Indian Ocean. The Mwata Yamvo of the west and his viceroy, the Mwata Kazembe of the east, effectively monopolized the slave trade of the heartland. As the Atlantic market grew, Lunda influence spread both north toward the forest and south into the dry plain of the upper Zambezi. In the early 19th century the court began to receive ambassadorial visits from representatives of the king of Portugal, and some years later echoes of the Mwata's greatness reached the Protestant explorer-missionaries of the far south, such as David Livingstone.

In the 18th century the Dutch were replaced by the French as the leading slave merchants on the north coast of the Congo region as the scale of the trade grew rapidly. Congo captives became the dominant population in Saint-Domingue, later called Haiti, which rose to be the richest of all the world's colonies and before 1791 the largest supplier of sugar. The slaves carried with them some of their cultural values and tried to reconstruct their communities under the shadow of the great plantation houses. Bantu vocabulary and personal names were added to the Creole speech of the Caribbean. Kongo religious practices were preserved in a nominally Christian colonial society when attempts were made to minimize the insecurity and suffering by worship and ritual. But, however much the slaves tried to reconstruct Central African society in the New World, their departure left a serious mark on the Old World. The scale of the French trade rose to about 10,000 men, women, and children each year. The demographic hemorrhage was felt in spreading ripples, and the already frail population of Central Africa was further weakened. Not until the outbreak of revolution in France, and later in Haiti, did the French trade begin to decline.

Although the Central African population had declined and did not begin to recover until the beginning of the 20th century, two new crops introduced to the region from the Americas enhanced the productive capacity of the land and helped Central Africans recover from the ravages of slaving. The first was corn (maize), which required the same agricultural skills as millet and so could be easily adopted. Corn had the advantage over millet that its grain was wrapped in an envelope of leaves that protected the crop from predatory birds. Corn also had higher yields than millet where soil and water were sufficient, which increased food production and partly compensated for the loss of field hands to the slavers. The second new crop was cassava, or manioc, a root crop easily adopted by

Also called manioc, mandioca, and yuca, cassava comes from the American tropics. It is a good source of dietary fibre as well as vitamin C, thiamin, folic acid, manganese, and potassium.

tuber farmers but more difficult for grain farmers to accept. It too was better protected from rodents—and even from marauders—than traditional crops. Cassava could be left in the ground when farmers had to flee in war and then recovered whole and edible on their return. To those unfamiliar with cassava, however, it could be dangerous, because the protective poisons in the plant, which made it inedible to vermin, had to be washed out before it was cooked for human consumption.

New crops from outside brought some small benefit to the region, but new diseases had the opposite effect. The growth of long-distance communication led to the spread of smallpox along the slave trails. It was a disease much feared both in the villages and on the slave ships. During serious periods of warfare and raiding, populations were weakened by famine and so easily fell prey to measles and pneumonia. Central Africa was also a malarial zone, although the disease was most deadly for Europeans. Equally dangerous to Africans, especially in the 20th century, were epidemics of sleeping sickness, which periodically spread through the region. As though this were not enough, Central Africa was attacked in the early 20th century by the world influenza pandemic. The already weakened population became thinner still and did not recover until well into the middle of the century.

The Central African slave trade continued into the 19th century, however. The Portuguese moved back into northern Central Africa when the French trade declined, and Brazil bought more slaves than ever before from Central Africa in the first half of the century, continuing to use slaves until the 1880s. Spain also entered the market to buy slaves for its surviving American colony in Cuba, where the tobacco industry combined the modernization of the railway age with the old plantation use of slaves.

The abolition movement helped to end the slave trade by the late 19th century, although slavery continued in Africa into the 20th century. While the end of four centuries of international slaving might have been expected to lead to a new era of freedom and opportunity in Central Africa, this did not happen. Instead, a whole new set of foreign forces began to penetrate the area. The first of these came from the long-delayed growth of international commerce on the northern border of the region.

EXPLOITATION OF IVORY

In the second half of the 19th century, the northern border of Central Africa was suddenly opened up to the impact of an intense new trade in ivory. Rapid prosperity in both Europe and North America had led to an increase in demand for ivory to make piano keys, billiard balls, knife handles, and ornamental carvings. Traders from Egypt and the old Ottoman Empire of North Africa went across the Sahara and up the Nile to cross into the upper reaches of the Congo basin, where elephants were still plentiful. In so doing, they severely disrupted local societies as they kidnapped local peoples to serve as bearers, servants, and concubines. The victims of the trading and hunting raids not only were used in the heavily armed and fortified ivory camps but also were taken away to be sold as slave girls in the harems of Constantinople or as water carriers in the streets of Cairo.

The second mobile frontier to intrude on Central Africa in the 19th century was in the east, and eventually it became as disruptive as the northern incursion. The first immigrants were long-distance traders from the Nyamwezi kingdom founded by Mirambo, who arrived in search of copper. They set up their own trading kingdom under Msiri and developed a large army of followers equipped with lances and bows. Msiri also trained a military elite of 2,000 men, whom he armed with guns bought on the east coast in exchange for ivory. Msiri's kingdom became one of the largest conquest states to be carved out in Central Africa. He adopted the administrative methods of the old Lunda kings, whose provinces he captured and whose governors he reappointed as his own agents and consuls. He also gained control of the old empire's eastern slave trade. In this field, however, Msiri had a powerful rival in the Swahili trade community, which had reached Central Africa from Zanzibar.

The Swahili traders and their Arab allies were involved with both the slave trade and the ivory trade. Their slaves were put to work on the spice plantations of Zanzibar or sold as pearl divers and domestic servants in the Arabian and Persian gulfs. The ivory went to the United States to buy calico, which was in great demand in the eastern Congo basin. One of the traders took the nickname "Americani" because his American calico was so famed. An even better-known Swahili merchant prince was Tippu Tib, who became the effective ruler of the Swahili towns on the upper reaches of the Congo River. His methods of trade were brutal. Villagers were forcibly rounded up into camps, often with great loss of life—as witnessed by Livingstone on his visit—and then ransomed by their relatives, who were sent out on hazardous elephant-trapping expeditions. The ivory trade thus disrupted the east as effectively as it disrupted the north. Worse still, the pattern of exploitation was one that was soon adopted by the first Europeans to enter the region. They also used capture and ransom to extract wealth from their victims. The first European ruler of the Congo, the Belgian king Leopold, appointed Tippu Tib his governor and gave him command of the east in recognition of his military and commercial achievements.

Tippu Tib was the most famous late 19th-century Arab trader in Central and eastern Africa. His chief interest was the ivory trade.

The great 19th-century scramble for ivory also brought disruption to Central Africa from the south in the years immediately preceding the colonial partition. The agents in the south were Chokwe hunters from Angola. They had been successful collectors of beeswax, and their trade had enabled them to build up armories of guns, which they eventually turned on their neighbours. They penetrated the heartland of the Lunda empire in the 1880s and destroyed the court. Their victims were sold on the Atlantic coast and were the last European-owned slaves on the old plantations of São Tomé. Their ivory went to the Portuguese after the crown had abandoned its restrictive monopoly on tusks and allowed private entrepreneurs to benefit from market forces. But when ivory became scarce and slaves were frowned upon, the Chokwe pioneered a new branch of trade that was to bring even greater horrors to the peoples of Central Africa. This was the search for red rubber, the sap of the wild rubber vine that grew throughout the forest and savanna galleries of the Congo basin. As the price of rubber rose with the development of the electrical and motor industries, so the rubber traders penetrated further into the communities of refugees who had sought to escape the disruptions of the last phase of the slave trade. It was the rubber trade that financed the first stage of formal colonial rule in Central Africa.

COLONIALISM

Before the race for partition, only three European powers—France, Portugal, and Britain—had territory in tropical Africa, located mainly in West Africa. However, the ground for eventual occupation of the interior of tropical Africa was being prepared by explorers, missionaries, and traders. But such penetration remained tenuous until the construction of railroads and the arrival of steamships on navigable waterways made it feasible for European merchants to dominate the trade of the interior and for European governments to consolidate conquests.

ESTABLISHMENT OF EUROPEAN COLONIES

The pioneer colonizer in Central Africa was Leopold II, king of the Belgians. The early attempts of his father, Leopold I, to found colonies in remnants of the Spanish empire in the Pacific or America had failed, and he therefore turned his attention to Central Africa, which was still little known to European geographers and therefore less intensely coveted than West or Southern Africa. He set up his colony (the Congo Free State) as a private, ostensibly humanitarian venture aimed at limiting the devastation of slaving and the liquor trade. To finance the venture, however, he rented out nation-size fiefs to commercial companies that were licensed to make a profit and pay tax and tribute to the colonizer-king. Companies such as the Anglo-Belgian India Rubber Company, the Antwerp Company, and the king's own Crown Domain took over the extraction of rubber from the Chokwe. Since the profits on rubber were low compared with ivory or slaves, great pressure had to be brought to bear to encourage newly subjected villagers to forsake their agricultural livelihoods and risk their lives in the forest to gather the vine sap. Military force was used, rubber collecting became compulsory, and defaulters were barbarically punished by having their limbs amputated. The rubber regime in the western Congo basin was no more benign than the ivory regime that Leopold adopted from the Swahili in the east.

The humanitarian protest against the rule of Leopold was led by traders who had lost access to their former sphere of interest, by missionaries who deplored the denial of human rights, and by a British diplomat who believed in political freedom. Roger (later Sir Roger) Casement publicized the atrocities in the Congo Free State to such good effect that in 1908 the Belgian government confiscated the colony from its own king in an attempt to put an end to the misrule of exploitation. However much other nations

Although Leopold II played a significant role in the development of the modern Belgian state, he was also responsible for widespread atrocities committed under his rule against his colonial subjects.

might have condemned Leopold's rule, rival colonizers were also keen to make their colonies profitable and did so by farming out concessions to private enterprise and turning a blind eye to the large-scale use of forced labour.

The most immediate rival to Leopold in creating instant new colonies was Otto von Bismarck, chancellor of the new German Empire. Most of the colonies he created were outside Central Africa, but he did succeed in laying claim to one tiny but richly populated corner on the mountainous border of East Africa. The old kingdoms of Rwanda and Burundi had thrived for centuries. The ruling class grew tall on the milk of its cattle and governed its farming subjects with imperious superiority. In the forest the old inhabitants continued to maintain their hunting lifestyle and, where possible, to escape the attentions of their neighbours. In the late 19th century Burundi underwent severe dislocation, with conflicts over the monarchy and rivalry between chiefs and kings. The Germans moved in from Tanganyika and tried to impose order. They also took over the more stable kingdom of Rwanda.

Burundi and Rwanda (as the mandate of Ruanda-Urundi) were awarded to Belgium after World War I, when Germany lost its colonies. Under the Belgian colonial administrators, the colony was reorganized in the late 1920s, with the result that most chiefs and subchiefs were eliminated. It would be overly simplistic to blame all of the region's post-colonial ethnic troubles on European ignorance of African culture, but such ignorance did contribute significantly to these problems. Assuming that ethnicity could be clearly distinguished by physical characteristics and then using the ethnic differences found in their own countries as models, Germany and especially Belgium created a system whereby the categories of Hutu and Tutsi were no longer fluid. The Tutsi—because of their generally lighter skin and greater height and as a result of European bias toward those physical characteristics—were considered superior to Hutu and given preference in local administration. Thus, power continued to be concentrated in the Tutsi minority.

Although the German intrusion into Central Africa from the east was slight and short-lived, a comparable French intrusion in the west led to the creation of a much bigger and more lasting equatorial empire. It was the work of the explorer-turned-governor Pierre Savorgnan de Brazza. The French presence was confined at first to former slaving beaches on the Congo coast and Libreville, a haven for freed slaves on the Gabon Estuary. Brazza aspired to join these coastal enclaves to the middle stretch of the Congo River, where the colonial capital was named Brazzaville in his honour. He also aspired to claim territory for France as far east as the upper regions of the Nile. Such an enterprise brought France into competition not only with Leopold, on the far bank of the river, but also with Britain, which had laid claim to the lower Nile in Egypt and wanted to protect the headwaters by conquering the upper Nile as well. The French were narrowly defeated in the race to the Nile (the Fashoda incident) but nevertheless gained imperial dominion over a huge stretch of northern Central Africa, which they called Ubangi-Shari and which later became the diamond-rich Central African Republic.

The problems that France faced in Central Africa were not materially different from those faced by Leopold. The territories were huge, thinly peopled, and poorly endowed with resources that could finance colonial administration and make a profit for the colonizing power. Transport was the greatest difficulty. Leopold went so far as to claim that the essence of colonization was the creation of a transport system. Both France and Leopold were handicapped by the rapids on the lower Congo River and so each had, at huge cost in money and men, to build a railway to reach the navigable middle river. Leopold used the famous British-American explorer Henry (later Sir

The Italian-born French explorer and colonial administrator Pierre Savorgnan de Brazza founded both the French (Middle) Congo (now the Republic of the Congo) and the city of Brazzaville.

Henry) Morton Stanley, the "Breaker of Rocks" (Bula Mutari), to mobilize the necessary forced labour to gain access to his territory. The French tried importing Chinese workers, who could be hired in Asia even more cheaply than local labour could be conscripted in Africa.

The French imitated Leopold, and also the British and Portuguese, by awarding concessions to colonial companies on the condition that they take responsibility for their own administration and infrastructure in return for the right to extract profits from subject peoples and conquered lands. The most notorious of the French colonial entrepreneurs made their money out of timber concessions. Only toward the end of the colonial period and after did French Equatorial Africa discover that it was rich in iron ore, petroleum, and uranium.

British influence in Central Africa was limited to the far northeast of the area, and was related to the British control of Egypt. By 1874 the Egyptians (themselves ruled by the Turkish Ottoman Empire) had conquered the entire Sudan region, including what are now Sudan and South Sudan. The slave trade was greatly expanded and pushed into what is now South Sudan. The various sub-Saharan African peoples of the south, who were primarily Christian and animist, were enslaved by the Muslim Arabs of the north. The hatred engendered by the slave trade still persists.

The Egyptians encouraged British interference in Sudan, and this aroused Muslim opposition to Egyptian rule. Muhammad Ahmad proclaimed himself the Mahdi (meaning the "divinely guided") and organized a resistance movement. His followers laid siege to Khartoum and overwhelmed Anglo-Egyptian forces on January 26, 1885. The Mahdi established a Muslim state, but he died of typhus five months after the fall of Khartoum. The Mahdist state continued under the rule of his successor, who was known as the Khalifah (meaning "caliph"). Meanwhile, the British had occupied Egypt, and they wanted to keep rival European powers out of the Nile Valley. Sudan had been under the rule of the Khalifah for about 12 years when the British invaded to protect the Nile from French forces. A decisive battle occurred at Omdurman on September 2, 1898, when the British—using machine guns— killed about 10,000 Mahdist fighters and lost only 48 of their own men. After the British conquest, Sudan was ruled jointly by the British and the Egyptians as Anglo-Egyptian Sudan.

ECONOMIC ORGANIZATION

The violent phase of Central African colonialism, involving the forced extraction of rubber, ivory, and timber, was followed by a more systematic phase of economic organization. One facet was the establishment of formal plantations on which to grow oil palms and rubber trees. These plantations required capital, machinery, and expensive foreign management. As a result, there was little margin left for adequate wages for workers. The recruitment of labour became the duty of the colonial state or its licensed agents. Some workers accepted the incentive of a cash wage to buy material goods or to accumulate the necessary social payments for marriage. Others were driven into the wage sector by the imposition of cash taxes, which could be met only by working for colonial enterprises. But some were recruited on a compulsory basis—not as convicts deserving of punishment but as subjects who needed to be "civilized" by submitting to a work regime imposed by the state.

Where plantations did not develop, the colonial state found a means of extracting wealth from free peasants. They introduced compulsory crops, most notably cotton—"*le coton du gouverneur.*" Forced cotton imposed severe hardships on farmers, who could not grow food for their families but instead had to clear land to sow cotton for the state. When the crop succeeded, they received a small payment. But much of the cotton regime was applied to marginal lands, where it often failed. The risk was borne by the victim, and famine resulted. The planting of cotton led to frequent protests and to harsh repression in Central Africa.

The largest industrial complex to develop in Central Africa was the mining industry of the copper belt in what is now far southeastern Congo (Kinshasa). Leopold had won a race with the British South African empire builder Cecil Rhodes to reach the copper mines and had conquered the kingdom of Msiri, killing the king in the process. The next challenge was to build a transport system that could carry machinery into the mining zone and export finished ingots. The politics of transport were the key to development in the high colonial period, as they had been in the early phase. Two railway lines ran to the Indian Ocean coast: one was built across German Africa to the port of Dar es Salaam and another through British Zambesia to the Portuguese port of Beira; a third railroad crossed Angola to the harbour of Lobito on the Atlantic. None of these, however, was under the control of the Belgians, who planned to create a national route to their own port of Matadi on the Congo estuary. To do so they had to use an expensive and complex mixture of rail and river steamers, and so the copper mines remained integrated in an international network of finance and transport. They also depended on neighbouring regions for their supply of coal and electricity. The industry was dominated by a concession company, the Union Minière du Haut-Katanga, which became almost as powerful as the colonial state itself. The two were interlocked in rivalry and mutual dependence, and the Belgian Congo was described as the "portfolio state" for its reliance on copper shares.

Two other mining zones added to the wealth of the colonial Congo: diamonds in the west and gold in the east. Between them the three mining zones were large-scale employers of unskilled labour. Some workers were temporary migrants who worked on contract and whose families subsisted on peasants' incomes during their absence. Much of the burden of colonialism fell on women, who became heads of households and managers of family farms when the men were taken to the mines. Part of the mine labour was supplied by migrants who moved permanently to the towns and became proletarian workers exclusively dependent on their wages. Among the townsmen, education and technical training became the road to economic advancement. The Belgian colonial system maintained a rigorous paternal structure, however, and, although more subjects became literate in Congo than in other colonies, few could aspire to higher skills or managerial posts. These positions were reserved for the white expatriate population.

THE CHURCH IN CENTRAL AFRICA

One distinctive feature of the colonial era in Central Africa was the role of the church. The state provided so few services that missions moved in to make up the deficit. The most famous of all missionaries was Albert Schweitzer, the Alsatian musician and theologian who became a physician and set up a hospital in the heart of French Equatorial Africa. British Baptists also played a major role in converting the people of the lower Congo area to Protestantism and providing them with basic education and minimal welfare services. When turmoil again hit the region at the end of the colonial period, it was the Baptists who brought services to the mass refugee camps. In the Belgian sphere the Roman Catholic Church took a high profile and eventually established a Catholic university through which to train not only colonial whites but also a small elite of black Africans. The rival to the state church was an independent black church, built in honour of the martyred preacher Simon Kimbangu, who spent

(CONTINUED ON THE NEXT PAGE)

(CONTINUED FROM THE PREVIOUS PAGE)

most of his life in a Belgian colonial prison. Later still, Central Africa became a prime zone of evangelism for the fundamentalist groups that sprang up in the United States in the last decades of the 20th century. When the postcolonial state withered, the churches took on greater formal and informal responsibilities for health and education and for communications and financial services in remote areas.

In Sudan, modernization was slow at first. Taxes were purposely kept light, and the government consequently had few funds available for development. In fact, the Sudan remained dependent on Egyptian subsidies for many years. Nevertheless, railway, telegraph, and steamer services were expanded, particularly in Al-Jazīrah, in order to launch the great cotton-growing scheme that remains today the backbone of Sudan's economy. In addition, technical and primary schools were established, including the Gordon Memorial College, which opened in 1902 and soon began to produce a Western-educated elite that was gradually drawn away from the traditional political and social framework.

THE END OF THE COLONIAL PERIOD

Sudan became the first part of Central Africa to win its independence on January 1, 1956. The colonial period in the rest of Central Africa came to an abrupt end in 1960. At a constitutional level, dramatic changes occurred. Both France and Belgium decided that they could not resist the winds of change with armed force. Once the black nationalists of West Africa had won the right to self-determination from Britain, it was not deemed possible to deny the same rights in Central Africa. New constitutions were therefore accepted, parliaments were elected, and flags were flown and anthems played. General Charles de Gaulle of France, whose path to power had led him to Brazzaville during World War II, became the hero of the new equatorial republics to which he granted independence. King Baudouin of the Belgians participated in the independence celebrations of Congo at Léopoldville (now Kinshasa) but managed to orchestrate his reception with less finesse. "Flag independence" in Central Africa, however, did not bring any real transformation to satisfy the high aspirations of former colonial subjects.

SUDAN

In 1936 Britain and Egypt had reached a partial accord in the Anglo-Egyptian Treaty that enabled Egyptian officials to return to the Sudan. Although the traditional Sudanese sheikhs and chiefs remained indifferent to the fact that they had not been consulted in the negotiations over this treaty, the educated Sudanese elite were resentful that neither Britain nor Egypt had bothered to solicit their opinions. Thus, they began to express their grievances through the Graduates' General Congress, which had been established as an alumni association of Gordon Memorial College and soon embraced all educated Sudanese. The organization demanded recognition by the British to act as the spokesman for Sudanese nationalism. In time the Congress split into two groups: a moderate majority, prepared to accept the good faith of the government, and a radical minority, led by Ismāʿīl al-Azharī, which turned to Egypt. Although the Sudanese government had crushed the initial hopes of the Congress, the British officials were aware of the power of nationalism and sought to introduce new institutions to associate the Sudanese more closely with the task of governing. An advisory council was established for the northern Sudan; in 1947 they instituted southern participation in the legislative council.

The creation of this council produced a strong reaction on the part of the Egyptian government, which in October 1951 unilaterally abrogated the Anglo-Egyptian Treaty of 1936 and proclaimed Egyptian rule over the Sudan. These ill-considered actions only managed to alienate the Sudanese from Egypt until the revolution in July 1952 placed men with more understanding of Sudanese aspirations in power in Cairo. On February 12, 1953, the Egyptian government signed an agreement with Britain granting self-government for the Sudan and self-determination within three years for the Sudanese. Elections for a representative parliament to rule the Sudan followed in November and December 1953. To the shock of many British officials and to the chagrin of the moderate Ummah (Nation) Party, which had enjoyed power in the legislative council for nearly six years, Ismāʿīl al-Azharī's National Unionist Party (NUP) won an overwhelming victory. Although Azharī had campaigned to unite the Sudan with Egypt, the realities of disturbances in the southern Sudan and the responsibilities of political power and authority ultimately led him to disown his own campaign promises and to declare Sudan an independent republic with an elected representative parliament on January 1, 1956.

The triumph of liberal democracy in Sudan was short-lived. Compared with the strength of tradition, which still shaped the life of the Sudanese, the liberalism imported from the West was a weak force, disseminated through British education and adopted by the Sudanese intelligentsia. At first parliamentary government had been held in high esteem as the symbol of nationalism and independence. But, at best, the parliament was a superficial instrument. Disillusioned with their experiment in liberal democracy, the Sudanese turned once again to authoritarianism.

THE FORMER FRENCH EQUATORIAL AFRICA

The experience of fighting alongside Charles de Gaulle's Free French forces during World War II raised the profile and the political consciousness of France's African colonies. After the war, the colonies felt the right to demand a more equitable relationship with France. The French government, realizing the need to introduce reform but reluctant to take any steps that might compromise its control over the colonies, responded by writing limited concessions into the new constitution of 1946. The

French colonial empire was renamed as the French Union, and its territories were given a token level of self-rule and allowed to elect a few representatives to the French National Assembly.

Although the 1946 constitution marked only minimal progress toward political participation for Africans, nationalists seized the moment. Later in the year, budding nationalist parties came together to form a unified political organization known as the Rassemblement Démocratique Africain (RDA; African Democratic Rally). The organization's president, Félix Houphouët-Boigny of Côte d'Ivoire, used his influence as a member of the National Assembly to win passage of the Loi Cadre (Outline Law) in 1956. The law reserved control of economic development, defense, and foreign policy within the union for France but gave responsibility for all other matters to the individual territories. Guinea's success encouraged the other French colonies to reconsider their positions, and they soon began to demand independence as well. By the end of 1960, the territories of Equatorial Africa had emerged as the independent nations of the Central African Republic (formerly Ubangi-Shari), Chad, Congo, and Gabon.

THE FORMER BELGIAN CONGO

This decentralization and regionalization of the colonial structure in the Belgian Congo created an ethnically divided and politically stifled African elite. Unlike many Africans under British and French colonial rule, the Congolese lacked a national ideology. The ethnic association of the Kongo people, however, was the basis for the formation of one of the first African political parties in the Congo, the Alliance des Ba-Kongo (ABAKO), under the leadership of Joseph Kasavubu. It was not until 1958 that the Mouvement Nationale Congolais (MNC) formed and began to work toward independence. Fast-growing political unrest led to independence on June 30, 1960, with Kasavubu as president and Patrice Lumumba as prime minister.

From the outset, turmoil wracked the newly independent country as Kasavubu and Lumumba struggled for control of the government. The lack of central authority exacerbated the disunity that existed throughout the Congo, as regional warlords vied with the official government for control of the country. In an attempt to gain foreign economic and military support to hold the country together, Lumumba turned to the United States and the powers of western Europe, but his overtures were rebuffed.

In this photo from 1960, Congolese protesters in Léopoldville (now known as Kinshasa) are taking part in a march over who would control the government of the newly independent Republic of the Congo.

He then turned to the Soviet Union. Eager to gain a foothold in Central Africa, the Soviet Union supplied military and economic aid to Lumumba, which he in turn used to attempt to put down revolts throughout the country. Wary of Lumumba's growing authority, Kasavubu appealed to the United States and Belgium for support against Lumumba, charging that the prime minister was turning the Congo over to the Soviet Union. As the two leaders fought for power, ethnic tension spread throughout the country. A secessionist movement evolved in Lubumbashi, the capital of the southeastern province of Shaba (now Katanga). Less than four months after gaining independence, the Congo began to slip into a state of anarchy. In September 1960 the army's chief of staff, Joseph Mobutu, took control of the country, ruling as a dictator who crushed all opposition for more than 30 years.

RWANDA AND BURUNDI

The traditional leaders of Burundi and Rwanda were denied legal status for a political party they formed in 1955. Three years later Unity for National Progress (Unité pour le Progrès National; UPRONA) was established in Burundi and in 1959 the *mwami* (Burundi's traditionally Tutsi king) was made a constitutional monarch. Legislative elections were held in 1961 and resulted in victory for UPRONA. Of the 64 legislative seats, the ethnically mixed party won 58, of which 22 were held by Hutu members of UPRONA. The party leader was Prince Rwagasore, a Tutsi and the eldest son of Mwami Mwambutsa. Rwagasore represented populist aspirations and was the strongest supporter of the monarchy. He became prime minister and formed a new government. His assassination on October 13, 1961, ushered in a crisis from which the country has struggled to recover ever since. Despite this crisis, Burundi became independent on July 1, 1962. Discord and violence have marked Burundi since independence. Although bloodshed has not occurred on the scale seen in Rwanda, ethnic conflict has resulted in hundreds of thousands of deaths and hundreds of thousands of people being displaced from their homes.

By the end of the Belgian trusteeship in 1962, Rwanda and Burundi had evolved radically different political systems. Rwanda had declared itself a republic in January 1961 and forced its monarch (*mwami*), Kigeri, into exile. Burundi, on the other hand, would retain the formal trappings of a constitutional monarchy until 1966. The Rwanda revolution was rooted partly in a traditional system of stratification based on an all-embracing "premise of inequality" and partly in a colonial heritage that greatly increased the oppressiveness of the few over the many. Tutsi hegemony was unquestionably more burdensome under Belgian rule than at any time prior to European colonization. By the end of World War II, a growing number of colonial civil servants and missionaries had come to recognize the legitimacy of Hutu claims against the ruling Tutsi minority. The proclamation of the republic a year and a half before the country acceded to independence testifies to the substantial support extended by the trusteeship authorities to the revolution.

What began as a peasant revolt in November 1959 eventually transformed itself into an organized political movement aimed at the overthrow of the monarchy and the vesting of full political power in Hutu hands. Under the leadership of Grégoire Kayibanda, Rwanda's first president, the Party for Hutu Emancipation (Parti du Mouvement de l'Emancipation du Peuple Hutu) emerged as the spearhead of the revolution. Communal elections were held in 1960, resulting in a massive transfer of power to Hutu elements at the local level. And in the wake of the coup (January 1961) in Gitarama in central Rwanda, which was carried off with the tacit approval of the Belgian authorities, an all-Hutu provisional government came into being. Therefore, by the time that independence was proclaimed in July 1962, the revolution had already run its course. Thousands of Tutsi began fleeing Rwanda, and by early 1964— following a failed Tutsi raid from Burundi—at least 150,000 were in neighbouring countries.

With the elimination of Tutsi elements from the political arena, north-south regional competition among Hutu politicians arose, reflecting the comparatively privileged position of those from the central and southern regions within the party, the government, and the administration. Regional tensions came to a head in July 1973, when a group of army officers from the north overthrew the Kayibanda regime in a bloodless coup and installed a northerner, Maj. Gen. Juvénal Habyarimana. Habyarimana gave a distinctly regional coloration to the institutions of the state during his 21 years in power, which ended only at his death in the 1994 plane crash that led to the genocide of April–July 1994.

CHAPTER FOUR

EASTERN AFRICA

• •

E astern Africa is the part of sub-Saharan Africa comprising two traditionally recognized regions: East Africa (made up of Kenya, Tanzania, and Uganda) and the Horn of Africa (made up of Somalia, Djibouti, Eritrea, and Ethiopia).

Eastern Africa consists largely of plateaus and has most of the highest elevations in the continent. The two most striking highlands are in Ethiopia and Kenya, respectively, where large areas reach elevations of 6,500 to 10,000 feet (2,000 to 3,000 metres). Twin parallel rift valleys that are part of the East African Rift System run through the region. The Eastern, or Great, Rift Valley extends from the Red Sea's junction with the Gulf of Aden southward across the highlands of Ethiopia and Kenya and continues on into Tanzania. The Western Rift Valley curves along the western borders of Uganda and Tanzania. Between the two rift valleys lies a plateau that comprises most of Uganda and western Tanzania and includes Lake Victoria. The volcanic massif of Kilimanjaro, the highest mountain in Africa, reaches 19,340 feet (5,895 metres) in northeastern Tanzania. The Horn of Africa, a major peninsular extension of the African mainland into the Arabian Sea, contains the vast lowland coastal plains of Somalia.

The climate of eastern Africa is generally tropical, though average temperatures tend to be reduced by the region's high elevations. Precipitation also is affected by varying elevation: Uganda, Tanzania, and western Kenya receive plentiful rainfall, while Somalia, eastern Ethiopia, and northeastern Kenya receive far less. The region's vegetation ranges from woodlands and grasslands in the wetter regions to thornbushes in semiarid areas.

Trading contacts between Arabia and the East African coast resulted in the establishment of numerous Asian and Arab trade settlements along the coast and in the interior prior to any contact with European colonial powers. The coastal trading centres were mainly Arab-controlled, and relations between the Arabs and their African neighbours appear to have been fairly friendly. After the arrival of the Portuguese

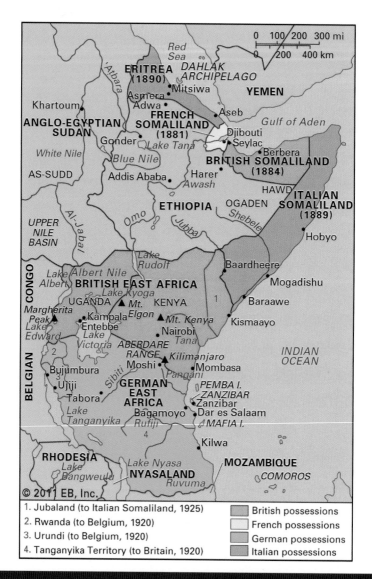

1. Jubaland (to Italian Somaliland, 1925)
2. Rwanda (to Belgium, 1920)
3. Urundi (to Belgium, 1920)
4. Tanganyika Territory (to Britain, 1920)

British possessions
French possessions
German possessions
Italian possessions

This map shows eastern Africa as it was partitioned by the imperial powers in about 1914. As you can see, the British, French, Germans, and Italians all established colonies there.

in the late 15th century, the position of the Arabs was gradually undermined, but the Portuguese made little attempt to penetrate into the interior. After the Portuguese expeditions, European exploration of Africa largely ceased for some two hundred years. By the 19th century, European countries had made their presence known again and, by the beginning of the 20th, all of eastern Africa—with the conspicuous exception of Ethiopia—had been colonized by the West.

EAST AFRICA

Although humans seem to have first developed in East Africa, in the three or four most recent millennia the key innovations in human evolution seem to have occurred elsewhere. However, the extensive agricultural revolution in East Africa during this time had the vital consequence that sizable populations grew up in areas of adequate rainfall in the interior, populations that could not be easily brushed aside by subsequent alien invaders. Over most of the last millennium, the history of coastal East Africa diverged from that of the East African interior. Unlike the interior, it was shaped by the region's history of maritime trade with the Indian subcontinent and the Arabian Peninsula.

COASTAL EAST AFRICA UNTIL 1856

By the middle of the last millennium, the ruling classes of the coastal towns were Muslims of mixed Arab and African descent who were mostly involved in trade. Beneath them were African laborers who were often slaves and a transient Arab population. The impetus in this society was Islamic rather than African. It was bound by sea to the distant Islamic world, whence immigrants still arrived to settle on the East African coast, to intermarry with local people, and to adopt the Swahili language. Mombasa (now in Kenya) became a very substantial town, as did Pate, in the Lamu islands. Other important towns were Malindi (also now in Kenya) and Kilwa (now in Tanzania). The islands of Zanzibar and Pemba, off the coast of what is now Tanzania, also became significant.

The Portuguese arrived in the area at the end of the 15th century and became the dominant power until they were driven out by the forces of the imam of Oman at the end of the 16th century. There ensued, after the Omani victory, a century during which, despite a succession of Omani incursions, the East African coast remained very largely free from the dominance of any outside power. Oman itself suffered an invasion by the Persians and was long distracted by civil conflict.

THE EARLY PORTUGUESE PRESENCE

Portuguese ships under Vasco da Gama arrived on the East African coast in 1498. The manifestly superior military and naval technology of the Portuguese and the greater unity of their command enabled them, in the following years, to mount assaults upon the ill-defended city-states. Within eight years they dominated the coast and the trade routes that led from there to India.

The Portuguese became skilled at playing one small state against another, but they did not immediately impose direct rule. This changed toward the end of the 16th century, however, when Turkish expeditions descending the northern coast with promises of assistance against the Portuguese encouraged the coast north of Pemba to revolt. This prompted the dispatch of Portuguese fleets from Goa, one of which, in 1589, sacked Mombasa and placed that city much more firmly under Portuguese control.

Portugal's chief interests were not imperial but economic. With Mombasa in their grip, the

(CONTINUED ON THE NEXT PAGE)

(CONTINUED FROM THE PREVIOUS PAGE)

Portuguese controlled the commercial system of the western Indian Ocean. Customs houses were opened at Mombasa and Pate, and ironware, weapons, beads, jewelry, cotton, and silks were imported. The main exports were ivory, gold, ambergris, and coral. There was a flourishing local trade in timber, pitch, rice, and cereals but few signs of any considerable traffic in slaves. Individual Portuguese traders often developed excellent relations with Swahilis in the coastal cities.

Though the Portuguese rode out local rebellions into the 17th century, their authority over a much wider area was undermined by the rise of new powers on the Persian Gulf. Portugal lost Hormuz to the Persians in 1622 and Muscat to the imam of Oman in 1650. The great Portuguese stronghold of Fort Jesus in Mombasa finally fell to Sayf ibn Sulṭān in December 1698. A few years later Zanzibar, the last of Portugal's allies in eastern Africa, also fell to the imam.

At the accession of Sayyid Saʿīd ibn Sulṭān in 1806, Omani weakness made the allegiance of the states along the East African coast little more than nominal, for at Mombasa the Mazarʾi family had set

up a virtually independent dynasty. In 1822 Saʿīd
sent an expedition that drove them from Pemba Island.
In subsequent years he became the main power in
the region and encouraged its economic development.
The increased economic activity that centred upon
the islands of Zanzibar and Pemba attracted an influx
of Western traders, of which the most important
were the Americans. They were the first Westerners
to conclude a trade agreement with Saʿīd (1833)
and the first also to establish a consul at Zanzibar
(1837). (Their prime achievement was to capture the
cloth trade to East Africa—so that cheap cotton cloth
thenceforth came to be known there as Americani.)
The British followed with a trade agreement in 1839
and a consul in 1841. The French made similar pro-
visions in 1844, and some Germans from the Hanse-
atic towns moved in at about the same time. British
trade never flourished (and in fact died away), but by
1856 the United States and France were both making purchases in East Africa of more than $500,000
a year, while exports to India, particularly British
India, were higher still. Some of the main items
of trade, such as ivory, were traditional, but copal,
sesame, cloves, cowries, hides, and coconut oil were
also important. Because of this increased activity,
Saʿīd's economy in due course became less dependent upon the export of slaves, and he therefore

showed himself more ready than he might otherwise have been to accept the so-called Hamerton Treaty of 1845, by which the export of slaves to his Arabian dominions was forbidden.

EAST AFRICA'S INTERIOR UNTIL 1856

The coast was never more than East Africa's fringe. Beyond the harsh *nyika*, or wilderness, which lay immediately inland and was nowhere pierced by a long, navigable river, thornbush country extended to the south, sometimes interspersed with pleasanter plains toward the centre, while to the north cooler forested highlands ran into harsher country. Westward lay the Great Rift Valley and, beyond, the regions of the great lakes whence the Nile ran northward through its usually impassable marshes.

The first Swahili-speaking traders from the east coast of Africa reached the country in the 1840s. Their object was to trade in ivory and slaves. Following the death of Sayyid Saʿīd in 1856, his erstwhile dominions on the coast of East Africa were split off from the imamate of Muscat. By 1873 the authority of the Āl Bū Saʿīdī sultans on Zanzibar itself had became complete, but this arose chiefly from the sultan's acceptance of the further measures against the East African slave trade pressed upon him by the British consul at his court. By the 1860s some 7,000 or so slaves were being sold annually in the Zanzibar slave market, but in 1873 a treaty with the British closed the market at Zanzibar, and Sultan Barghash, by two proclamations in 1876, reduced the export from the mainland to a trickle. As it happened, however, there was then a final period of unprecedented slaving on the mainland, where the trade in slaves had generally been closely connected with the trade in ivory and the demand for porters was still considerable.

COLONIALISM

Suggestions that he might at this time establish his dominion over the East African interior prompted Sultan Barghash to send a Baloch force to Tabora, but the idea was never pursued. A comparable notion, however, led Khedive Ismāʿīl Pasha of Egypt to appoint in 1869 the Englishman Samuel White Baker as governor of the Equatorial Province of the Sudan, so that Baker might carry the Egyptian flag to the East African lakes. Though Baker reached as far south as the kingdom of Bunyoro in 1872, he was soon obliged to leave. His successor, Charles George Gordon, proposed to circumvent both

Sultan Barghash was a shrewd and ambitious ruler. For most of his reign, he looked to Britain for protection and assistance but eventually saw his domains divided between Germany and his former protector.

Bunyoro and nearby Buganda by going straight up the Nile's banks. But Mutesa I, *kabaka* of Buganda, frustrated Gordon's efforts on the Nile, and by the early 1880s, with bankruptcy in Egypt and the Mahdist revolt in the Sudan, only remnants of the Egyptian enterprise remained.

The Egyptian incursion had been the climax to the search by many European explorers for the headwaters of the Nile—a quest that had obsessed the later years of the Scottish missionary David Livingstone and had prompted the discovery in 1858 of Lake Tanganyika by the English expedition of Richard Burton and John Hanning Speke. Speke returned first to discover Lake Victoria in 1858 and then with James Grant in 1862 became the first white man to set eyes on the source of the Nile, which Speke named Ripon Falls. By circumnavigating Lake Victoria 12 years later, Henry Morton Stanley stilled the controversy that had ensued in Europe over Speke's claim.

MISSIONARY ACTIVITY

The revelations of these explorers, the example of David Livingstone, concern in western Europe over the East African slave trade, and the Roman Catholic and evangelical fervour that existed there inspired the invasion of the East African interior by a motley collection of Christian missionary enterprises. Johann Ludwig Krapf and Johannes Rebmann of the Church Missionary Society, who had worked inland from Mombasa and had, in the 1840s and '50s, journeyed to the foothills of Mount Kenya and Kilimanjaro, were followed by a British Methodist mission. Roman Catholic missionaries reached Zanzibar in 1860 and settled at Bagamoyo in 1868. An Anglo-Catholic mission first tried to establish itself in the Shire highlands, then in 1864 transferred to Zanzibar. Anglican missionaries arriving in Buganda in the mid-1870s at the request of Kabaka Mutesa were soon followed by Catholic White Fathers—there and elsewhere on Zanzibar's Tabora route—while the London Missionary Society sent men both to Unyamwezi and to Lake Tanganyika.

There were, of course, a number of localized religious movements among the peoples of East Africa during the 19th century. These included the Mbari cult among the Nyakyusa, the Nyabingi in Rwanda, and the Yakany movement north of Mount Ruwenzori. None of them, however, spread in quite the way that the Chwezi movement had earlier. Islam, on the other hand—spread widely at the instance of the Zanzibari traders and long established on the coast—had secured a scattering of converts in the interior as in the key kingdom of Buganda.

This was the scene onto which Christian missionaries first entered. Although by 1885 there were nearly 300 of them in East Africa, they did not initially win many converts, and those they at first obtained came only from among freed slaves and refugees from local wars. After 1880, however, they made important conversions in Buganda, and by the end of the century Christianity was spreading in the Lake Victoria area over most of the region in which the Chwezi movement had previously percolated—and before very long over a much larger area as well.

PARTITION BY GERMANY AND BRITAIN

Philanthropic, commercial, and eventually imperialist ventures followed these evangelical endeavours. Nothing of great moment, however, occurred until 1885, when a German, Carl Peters, riding a tide of diplomatic hostility between Germany and Britain in Europe, secured the grant of an imperial charter for his German East Africa Company. With this the European scramble for Africa began. In east-central Africa the key occurrence was the Anglo-German Agreement of 1886, by which the two parties agreed that their spheres of influence in East Africa should be divided by a line running from south of Mombasa, then north of Kilimanjaro to a point on the eastern shore of Lake Victoria. This began the extraordinary process by which the territories and subsequently the nations of East Africa were blocked out first upon the maps far away in Europe and only later upon the ground in East Africa itself. The agreement put the area to the north (most of modern Kenya) under British influence and the area to the south (Tanganyika; modern mainland Tanzania) under German influence. The Anglo-German Agreement of 1890 placed additional territory (most of modern Uganda) under British influence.

Kenya was proclaimed a British protectorate in 1895 and a crown colony in 1920. Most of what is now Uganda was formally proclaimed a British protectorate in 1894, with additional areas being added to the protectorate in the following years. Tanganyika was declared a German protectorate in 1891. During World War I, Britain captured the German holdings, which became a British mandate in 1920. Britain retained control of Tanganyika after World War II when it became a United Nations trust territory.

Tanganyika gained independence in 1961 and in 1964 merged with Zanzibar, later taking the name

Tanzania. Uganda gained its independence in 1962, and Kenya became fully independent in 1963.

TANZANIA

Constitutionally, the most important immediate postwar development was the British government's decision to place Tanganyika under United Nations trusteeship (1947). Under the terms of the trusteeship agreement, Britain was called upon to develop the political life of the territory, which, however, only gradually began to take shape in the 1950s. In 1953 Julius Nyerere was elected president of the Tanganyika African Association (TAA), an organization made up mainly of African civil servants, which had been formed in Dar es Salaam in 1929. In early 1954 Nyerere and his associates transformed the TAA from a social organization to a political one, and later the same year the TAA became the Tanganyika African National Union (TANU), with the stated aims of self-government and independence.

The first two African members had been nominated to the Legislative Council in December 1945. This number was subsequently increased to four, with three Asian nonofficial members and four Europeans. An official majority was retained. In an important advance in 1955, the three groups were given parity of representation on the unofficial side of the council with 10 nominated members each, and for a time it seemed as if this basis would persist. The first elections to the unofficial side of the council (in 1958 and 1959), however, enabled TANU to show its strength, for even among the European and Asian candidates, only those supported by TANU were elected.

A constitutional committee in 1959 unanimously recommended that after the elections in 1960 a large majority of the members of both sides of the council be Africans and that elected members form the basis of the government. In the 1960 Legislative Council elections, TANU and its allies were again overwhelmingly victorious, and when Tanganyika became independent on December 9, 1961, Nyerere became its first prime minister. The next month, however, he resigned from this position in order to devote his time to writing and to synthesizing his views of government and of African unity; he was succeeded by Rashidi Kawawa. One of Nyerere's more important works was a paper called *Ujamaa— the Basis for African Socialism*, which later served as the philosophical basis for the Arusha Declaration of 1967.

On December 9, 1962, Tanganyika adopted a republican constitution, and Nyerere became executive president of the country. The next month, he announced that in the interest of national unity and economic development, TANU had decided that Tanganyika would now be a one-party state. Nyerere's administration was challenged in 1964; an army mutiny was suppressed in January only after the president reluctantly sought the assistance of British marines.

Although TANU was the only legal party, voters in each constituency were often offered a choice between more than one TANU candidate in parliamentary elections. That this arrangement amounted to something more than lip service to the idea of democracy was demonstrated in 1965 and in subsequent elections when, although Nyerere was reelected again and again as the sole candidate for president, a considerable number of legislators, including cabinet ministers, lost their seats.

On December 10, 1963, Zanzibar achieved independence as a member of the Commonwealth. In January 1964 the Zanzibar government was overthrown by an internal revolution, Sayyid Jamshid ibn Abdullah (who had succeeded to the sultanate in July 1963 on his father's death) was deposed, and a republic was proclaimed. Although the revolution was carried out by only about 600 armed men under the leadership of the communist-trained "field marshal" John Okello, it won considerable support from the African population. Thousands of Arabs were massacred in riots, and thousands more fled the island. Sheikh Abeid Amani Karume, leader of the ASP, was installed as president of the People's Republic of Zanzibar and Pemba. Sheikh Abdulla Kassim Hanga was appointed prime minister, and Abdul Raḥman Mohammed ("Babu"), leader of the new left-wing Umma (The Masses) Party (formed by defectors from the ZNP), became minister for defense and external affairs. Pending the establishment of a new constitution, the cabinet and all government departments were placed under the control of a Revolutionary Council of 30 members, which was also vested with temporary legislative powers. Zanzibar was proclaimed a one-party state. Measures taken by the new government included the nationalization of all land, with further powers to confiscate any immovable property without compensation except in cases of undue hardship.

On April 26, 1964, the two countries merged to form the United Republic of Tanganyika and Zanzibar, with Nyerere as president and Karume as first vice president. The nascent country was renamed the United Republic of Tanzania in October 1964. Despite unification, for years Zanzibar continued to pursue its own policies, paying little attention to mainland practices.

UGANDA

In the late 1950s, as a few political parties emerged, the African population concentrated its attention on achieving self-government, with focus on the Legislative Council. The kingdom of Buganda intermittently pressed for independence from Uganda, which raised the question of the protectorate's future status. Discussions in London in 1961 led to full internal self-government in March 1962. Benedicto Kiwanuka, a Roman Catholic Ganda who was formerly chief minister, became the first prime minister, but in the elections in April 1962 he was displaced by Milton Obote, a Lango (Langi) who headed the Uganda Peoples Congress (UPC) party. At further discussions in London in June 1962, it was agreed that Buganda should receive a wide degree of autonomy within a federal relationship. Faced with the emergence of Obote's UPC, which claimed support throughout the country apart from Buganda, and of the Democratic Party (DP), which was based in Buganda and led by Kiwanuka, conservative Ganda leaders set up their own rival organization, Kabaka Yekka (KY), "King Alone."

Uganda became independent on October 9, 1962, although it was divided politically on a geographic as well as an ethnic basis. By accepting a constitution that conceded what amounted to federal status to Buganda, Obote contrived an unlikely alliance with the Ganda establishment. Together the UPC and KY were able to form a government with Obote as prime minister and with the DP in opposition. Obote agreed to replace the British governor-general by appointing Mutesa II as the country's first president in an attempt to unify the alliance further, but this move was unsuccessful. Although Obote was able to win over some of the members of the KY and even of the DP so that they joined the UPC, tension grew steadily between the *kabaka* on the one hand and the UPC on the other. The Ganda leaders particularly resented their inability to dominate a government composed mainly of members of other ethnic groups. There were also divisions within the UPC, because each member of parliament owed his election to local ethnic supporters rather than to his membership in a political party. Those supporters frequently put pressure on their representatives to redress what they saw as an imbalance in the distribution of the material benefits of independence.

Faced with this dissatisfaction among some of his followers and with increasingly overt hostility in Buganda, Obote arrested five of his ministers and suspended the constitution in 1966. Outraged, the Ganda leaders ordered him to remove his government from the kingdom. Obote responded by sending troops under the leadership of Colonel Idi Amin to arrest the *kabaka*, who escaped to England, where he died in 1969. When Obote imposed a new republican constitution—appointing himself executive president, abolishing all the kingdoms, and dividing Buganda into administrative districts—he also lost the support of the peoples of southwestern Uganda. Internal friction subsequently grew in intensity, fostered by mutual suspicion between the rival groups, by assassination attempts against the president, and by the increasingly oppressive methods employed by the government to silence its critics.

At independence the export economy was flourishing without adversely affecting subsistence agriculture, and the economy continued to improve, largely because of the high demand and high prices for coffee. To answer accusations that the profits from exports did not benefit the producers enough, Obote attempted in 1969 to distribute the benefits from the prospering economy more widely. To this end he published a "common man's charter," which focused on removing the last vestiges of feudalism by having the government take a majority holding in the shares of the larger, mainly foreign-owned companies. In order to unite the country more firmly, he also produced a plan for a new electoral system in 1970 that would require successful candidates for parliament to secure votes in constituencies outside their home districts.

These proposals met with a cynical response in some quarters, but the government was overthrown before they could be put into effect. Obote had relied heavily on the loyalty of Idi Amin, but Amin had been building support for himself within the army by recruiting from his own Kakwa ethnic group in the northwest. The army, which had previously been composed of Acholi and their neighbours, Obote's own Lango people, now became sharply divided. Simultaneously, a rift developed between Obote and Amin, and in January 1971 Amin took advantage of the president's absence from the country to seize power.

KENYA

In 1944 Kenya became the first East African territory to include an African on its Legislative Council. The number was increased to two in 1946, four in 1948, and eight in 1951, although all were appointed by the governor from a list of names submitted by local governments. This, however, did not satisfy African demands for political equality. While the East African Association had been banned after Thuku's arrest, a new organization, the Kikuyu Central Association, emerged with Jomo Kenyatta as its general secretary beginning in 1928. Kenyatta, who advocated a peaceful transition to African majority rule, traveled widely in Europe and returned in 1946 to become the president of the Kenya African Union (KAU; founded in 1944 as the Kenya African Study Union), which attempted to gain a mass African following. There were, however, Africans in the colony who felt that Kenyatta's tactics were not producing enough concrete results. One such group, which advocated a violent approach, became known as the Mau Mau. The actions attributed to the Mau Mau caused the colonial government to proclaim a state of emergency from October 1952 until 1960 and also resulted in a massive relocation of Africans, particularly Kikuyu. Kenyatta and other Africans were charged with directing the Mau Mau movement and sentenced in 1953 to seven years' imprisonment; Kenyatta was released from prison in 1959 but was then confined to his home.

Jomo Kenyatta was the chief spokesman for Kenya's pursuit of independence for 30 years. He later became the country's first prime minister.

Numerous social and economic changes resulted either directly or indirectly from the Mau Mau uprising. A land-consolidation program centralized the Kikuyu into large villages. This plan was also extended to the area near Lake Victoria in the Nyanza province, and many thousands of Africans in Nairobi were re-settled in rural detention camps. At the same time, the Swynnerton Plan (a proposal to strengthen the development of African agriculture) provided Africans more opportunities to cultivate cash crops such as coffee. Throughout the 1950s, foreign investment in Kenya continued, and limited industrial development occurred along with agricultural expansion.

Although the leadership of the KAU had been arrested, the party was not immediately banned, because the government hoped that new party leadership might provide a more moderate approach. However, this was not forthcoming, and the party was banned by mid-1953; African political organizations were not allowed again until 1960. The Kenya African National Union (KANU), founded in May of that year and favouring a strong centralized government, was built around Kenyatta, who was still in detention. Nevertheless, in June two of KANU's founding members, Ronald Ngala and Daniel arap Moi, created their own organization, the Kenya African Democratic Union (KADU). KADU's position was that ethnic interests could best be addressed through a decentralized government; it was also concerned about Kikuyu domination. KANU won more seats than KADU in elections held in February 1961, but both parties called for the release of Kenyatta, who was finally freed from house detention in August. A coalition government of the two parties was formed in 1962, and after elections in May 1963 Kenyatta became prime minister under a constitution that gave Kenya self-government. Following further discussions in London, Kenya became fully independent on December 12, 1963. A year later, when Kenya became a republic (with Kenyatta as its first president and Oginga Odinga as vice president), most KADU members had transferred their allegiance to KANU, and KADU ceased to exist.

THE HORN OF AFRICA

The history of the Horn of Africa has largely been dominated by Ethiopia and has been characterized by struggles between Muslim and other herdsmen and Christian farmers for resources and living space. The Christians mostly spoke Semitic languages and the Muslims Cushitic tongues. Although these languages were derived from the same Afro-Asiatic stock, the more apparent differences between the peoples often were excuses for war, which, by the end of the 20th century, was waged under the banner of nationalism and Marxism-Leninism.

REVIVAL OF THE ETHIOPIAN EMPIRE

By the late 19th century the northernmost Oromo had been assimilated into Christian culture, and Abyssinia's national unity had been restored after a century of feudal anarchy that ended with the accession of Yohannes IV in 1872. Yohannes forced the submission of Ethiopia's princes, repulsed Egyptian expansionism in 1875–76, pushed back Mahdist invasions in 1885–86, and limited the Italians to the Eritrean coast. Meanwhile, the ambitious King Menilek II of Shewa began a reconquest of Ethiopia's southern and eastern peripheries in order to acquire commodities to sell for the weapons and ammunition he would need in his fight for the Solomonid crown. Italian adventurers, scientists, and missionaries helped organize a route, outside imperial control, that took Shewan caravans to the coast, where Menilek's ivory, gold, hides, and furs could be sold for a sizable (and untaxed) profit.

The economy of the Red Sea region had been stimulated by the opening of the Suez Canal, by the establishment of a British base in Aden, and by the opening of a French coaling station at Obock on the Afar coast. Britain sought to close off the Nile valley to the French by facilitating Rome's aspirations in the Horn. Thus, after 1885, Italy occupied coastal positions in Ethiopia and in southern Somalia. This limited the French

Menilek II expanded Ethiopia almost to its present-day borders, repelled an Italian invasion in 1896, and carried out a program of modernization.

to their mini-colony, leaving the British in control of ports in northern Somalia from which foodstuffs were exported to Aden. After Yohannes' death in March 1889, the Italians hoped to translate a cordial relationship with the new emperor, Menilek, into an Ethiopian empire.

On May 2, 1889, Menilek signed at Wichale (known as Ucciali to the Italians) a treaty of peace and amity with Italy. The Italians' famous mistranslation of Article XVII of the Treaty of Wichale provided them with an excuse to declare Ethiopia a protectorate. To Italy's dismay, the new emperor promptly wrote to the great powers, rejecting Rome's claim. Since neither France nor Russia accepted the new protectorate status, Ethiopia continued to acquire modern weapons from these countries through Obock. When, by 1894–95, Italy not only refused to rescind its declaration but also reinforced its army in Eritrea and invaded eastern Tigray, Menilek mobilized.

In late February 1896 an Ethiopian army of approximately 100,000 men was encamped at Adwa in Tigray, facing a much smaller enemy force some miles away. The Italians nevertheless attacked and were defeated on March 1, 1896, in what became known to Europeans as the Battle of Adwa. Menilek immediately withdrew his hungry army southward with 1,800 prisoner-hostages, leaving Eritrea to Rome in the hope that peace with honour would be restored quickly. On October 26, 1896, Italy signed the Treaty of Addis Ababa, conceding the unconditional abrogation of the Treaty of Wichale and recognizing Ethiopia's sovereign independence.

During the next decade, Menilek directed Ethiopia's return into the southern and western regions that had been abandoned in the 17th century. Most of the newly incorporated peoples there lived in segmented societies, practiced animal husbandry or cultivation with digging stick or hoe, followed traditional religions or Islam, and spoke non-Semitic languages. In practically every way but skin colour, the northerners were aliens. Their superior weapons and more complex social organization gave them a material advantage, but they also were inspired by the idea that they were regaining lands that had once been part of the Christian state. Menilek and his soldiers believed that they were on a holy crusade to restore Ethiopia to its historic grandeur, but they did not realize that they were participating in Europe's "scramble for Africa" and that they were creating problems among nationalities that would afflict the Horn of Africa throughout the 20th century.

THE BIRTH OF SOMALI NATIONALISM

About 1900 the first of these problems erupted in Somali-inhabited regions, under the leadership of Sayyid Maxamed Cabdulle Xasan. The rebellion was directed at the British, Italians, and Ethiopians, whom Maxamed regarded equally as oppressors and infidels. Indeed, these powers admitted their collusion by collaborating militarily against the sayyid and his forces from 1901 to 1904, forcing him to sue for peace and to withdraw into a remote and unadministered area of Italian Somaliland. By 1908 he was again on the attack, this time causing a massive civil war, during which tens of thousands of Somali clansmen died. The Italians and the British chose not to intervene, preferring to let Somali kill Somali, and limited their activities to the coast. It was not until 1920 that British air power ran the sayyid to ground, forcing him to flee into the Ogaden, where he died on December 21, 1920.

Maxamed pioneered the traditions of modern Somali nationalism, which combined Islam and anti-imperialism in a movement that sought to transcend clan divisions and make all Somali aware that they shared a common language, religion, way of life, and destiny. The Somali were further informed about their potential unity by, ironically, their Italian colonizers.

ITALIAN RULE

Despite the defeat at Adwa, Rome had not abandoned its dream of an Ethiopian empire. To this end, it worked hard at economic penetration but was invariably frustrated. More successful was its infiltration from Somalia into the adjacent Ogaden, where colonial troops seized strategic wells and posed as the protectors of Islam and the Somali people. By 1932 this advance alarmed Emperor Haile Selassie I, who was building a modern state in order to safeguard Ethiopia's independence.

As regent to Empress Zauditu from 1916 to 1930, and afterward as monarch, Haile Selassie had worked to reform the economy, government, communications, and military. His success was recognized early, on September 28, 1923, when Ethiopia entered the League of Nations. These achievements presaged a modern Ethiopian state that would block Rome's colonial plans and perhaps even undermine its position in the Horn of Africa. The potential threat of such a state, as well as considerations of European politics, led to the Italo-Ethiopian War, which began in the Ogaden, in December 1934, with a confrontation between Italian and Ethiopian soldiers at the water holes of Welwel.

Rome used Somalia and Eritrea as bases from which to launch its attack in October 1935. The issue was never in doubt; Haile Selassie had neither the armaments nor the disciplined troops necessary to fight the modern war that Italy mounted. In May 1936, after a terrible war that featured aerial bombardment and poison gas, he went into exile, and Italy proclaimed an East African empire consisting of Ethiopia, Eritrea, and its colony of Somalia.

The new regime, ignoring Ethiopia's traditional political organization, enlarged Eritrea to incorporate most of Tigray and placed the Ogaden in Somalia. In August 1940, after Rome had declared war against the Allies, the Italians marched north and occupied British Somaliland for seven months until dislodged by an Anglo-Ethiopian victory in the Horn of Africa. In 1942 and 1944 Anglo-Ethiopian treaties left the Ogaden under British rule for the duration of World War II, although Addis Ababa's sovereignty over the region was acknowledged. The British governed both Somalilands from a single city, Berbera, continuing the unification of the two territories.

PAN-SOMALISM

The Italians left Somaliland with an administrative infrastructure, communications, and towns, and the southern centres became incubators of pan-Somali ideas, which were quickly transmitted to their northern compatriots. The British allowed their subjects relative political freedom, and on May 13, 1943, the Somali Youth Club was formed in Mogadishu. Devoted to a concept of Somali unity that transcended ethnic considerations, the club quickly enrolled religious leaders, the gendarmerie, and the junior administration. By 1947, when it became the Somali Youth League, most of Somaliland's intelligentsia was devoted to pan-Somalism. This view was echoed in the British government's idea of Greater Somalia—a notion that was anathema to Ethiopia.

After his return to Addis Ababa in May 1941, Haile Selassie worked consistently to restore Ethiopia's sovereignty and to fend off British colonial encirclement and the isolation of his state. He regarded British activities in Somaliland as subversive and turned to the United States, which he concluded would be the dominant postwar power, to balance the geopolitical threat. American lend-lease and other assistance permitted Ethiopia to rebuff Britain and

Haile Selassie I was proclaimed the emperor of Ethiopia in 1930. Haile Selassie continued to rule until he was deposed by a military coup in 1974.

to secure the return of the Ogaden in 1948. The vision of Greater Somaliland, however, dominated Somali political programs in subsequent years.

ERITREAN NATIONALISM

Another fixed idea, that of Eritrean independence, also derived from the Italian years. Partisans here argued that Eritrea had evolved modern social and economic patterns and expectations from its colonial experience and, between 1941 and 1952, from the political freedoms allowed by the relatively liberal British military administration. While some Eritreans, especially Muslims and intellectuals, held these views in the 1940s, the idea of union with Ethiopia attracted the largely Christian population in the highlands—

arguably the colony's majority. The Christians joined the Unionist Party, sponsored by the Ethiopian government, which simultaneously sought international support for regaining its coastal province. The Ethiopians were assisted by an international fact-finding commission that visited Eritrea in late 1948 and concluded that there was no national consciousness to nourish statehood and that its backward agriculture, crude industrial base, and poor natural resources would not sustain independence. The commission recommended some form of dependency—a decision ultimately referred to the United Nations, where the United States was the most influential power.

Washington was concerned about retaining control of a communications station near the Eritrean city of Asmera (now Asmara), which beamed intelligence information from the Middle East to the Pentagon, and it decided to support Ethiopia's claim to Eritrea in return for a formal base treaty. With U.S. leadership, the United Nations agreed to a federation of Ethiopia and Eritrea, which came into being in 1952. One year later, responding to growing Soviet influence in Egypt, Washington decided to provide Ethiopia military and economic aid. The United States subsequently became Ethiopia's main supplier of capital, expertise, and technology as well as military training, equipment, and munitions—a relationship that ultimately drove Somalia into an alliance with the Soviet Union.

SOMALIA IRREDENTA

The Mogadishu government became independent on July 1, 1960. Its flag was dominated by a star, three points of which represented Djibouti, the Somali-inhabited northern region of Kenya, and the Ethiopian Ogaden. Together, these made up Somalia irredenta. In the Ogaden, young men organized themselves into clandestine fighting units, heeding Mogadishu's constant radio broadcasts to prepare for a war of liberation. In February 1963, the Ethiopian government sought to introduce a head tax to help sustain development efforts in the Ogaden. Somali nomads vigorously resisted the tax and rebelled, supported by the armed bands and then, in the fall of 1963, by Somalian troops. In November Mogadishu signed a military assistance pact with the Soviet Union, which undertook to equip a 20,000-man army. Shocked, the Ethiopians attacked Somalian border posts and adjacent towns in January 1964 and, after hard fighting, forced a cease-fire. Subsequent negotiations, however, were unable to resolve the differences between Somalia's goal of uniting all its compatriots and Ethiopia's need to retain its national integrity—as it was doing in Eritrea.

CHAPTER FIVE

SOUTHERN AFRICA

• •

Southern Africa may be considered as a single large culture area. It is the southernmost region of the African continent, comprising the countries of Angola, Botswana, Lesotho, Malawi, Mozambique, Namibia, South Africa, Swaziland, Zambia, and Zimbabwe. Most of it consists of open and dry savanna grasslands: the northwest contains the edges of the Congo forests; the southwest is very arid; and the coastline of South Africa and Mozambique is fertile, most of it with a subtropical or Mediterranean climate.

In Southern Africa, the intercolonial rivalries chiefly involved the British, the Portuguese, the South African Republic of the Transvaal, the British-backed Cape Colony, and the Germans. The acquisitive drive was enormously stimulated by dreams of wealth generated by the discovery of diamonds in Griqualand West and gold in Matabeleland. Encouraged by these discoveries, Cecil Rhodes (heading the British South Africa Company) and other entrepreneurs expected to find gold, copper, and diamonds in the regions surrounding the Transvaal, among them Bechuanaland, Matabeleland, Mashonaland, and Trans-Zambezia. In the ensuing struggle, which involved the conquest of the Nbele and Shona peoples, Britain obtained control over Bechuanaland and, through the British South Africa Company, over the areas later designated as the Rhodesias and Nyasaland. At the same time, Portugal moved inland to seize control over the colony of Mozambique. It was clearly the rivalries of stronger powers, especially the concern of Germany and France over the extension of British rule in Southern Africa, that enabled a weak Portugal to have its way in Angola and Mozambique.

EUROPEAN AND AFRICAN INTERACTION (15TH–18TH CENTURY)

The first Europeans to enter Southern Africa were the Portuguese, who from the 15th century edged their way around the African coast in the hope of outflanking Islam, finding a sea route to the riches of India, and discovering additional sources of food. They reached the Kongo kingdom in northwestern Angola in 1482–83.

THE PORTUGUESE

Initially the southeastern coast was of less interest to the Portuguese than west-central Africa. Within a few years, however, they had seized its wealthy but divided cities and had established themselves at Moçambique and Sofala, which soon became key ports of call for ships on the way to India.

The Portuguese conquests led to the economic and cultural decline of the east coast cities. Yet the newcomers faced resistance from coastal communities throughout the 16th century, and the profits they expected from the gold trade failed to materialize. In an attempt to control the trade, the Portuguese expanded into the Zambezi valley about 1530. However the Portuguese never had the resources to really control the interior.

From the beginning of the 17th century, the Portuguese faced increasingly severe competition from Dutch and British ships in the Indian Ocean, while north of Cape Delgado the Arabs also took advantage of Portuguese weakness. In 1631 a series of revolts began on the east coast; by the beginning of the 18th century the Portuguese had been driven from the coast north of the Rovuma River. The Portuguese then turned their attention southward, where they had traded at Delagoa Bay with the local Tsonga inhabitants since the mid 16th century. They were unable to establish themselves at the bay permanently, however, and through the 18th century Dutch, English, and Austrian ships competed for the local ivory while North American whalers also traded there for food and cattle. Local chiefdoms vied for this market, and this competition contributed to the buildup of larger states in the hinterland of Delagoa Bay from the mid 18th century. Doubtless there was also trade in slaves, although the numbers seem to have remained relatively small before the 19th century.

THE DUTCH AT THE CAPE

Apart from the Portuguese enclaves in Angola and Mozambique, the only other area of European settlement in Southern Africa in the 17th and 18th centuries was the Dutch settlement at the Cape of Good Hope. In the late 16th century the Cape had become a regular port of call for the crews of European ships, who found local people (Khoekhoe) ready to barter cattle in exchange for iron, copper, beads, tobacco, and brandy. By the mid 17th century Khoekhoe intermediaries traded far into the interior. These trade relationships profoundly affected the nature of contact between the Khoekhoe and the Dutch.

In 1652 the Dutch East India Company dispatched Commander Jan van Riebeeck and 125 men to set up a provisioning station at the Cape. This outpost soon grew into a colony of settlement. In 1657 the company released a number of its servants as free burghers (citizens) in order to cultivate land and herd cattle on its behalf. Slaves arrived the next year via a Dutch ship, which had captured them from a Portuguese vessel bound from Angola to Brazil. Thereafter slaves continued to arrive at the Cape from Madagascar and parts of western and eastern Africa. Although the company prohibited the enslavement of the local inhabitants, in order to protect the cattle trade, the loosely organized Khoekhoe were soon undermined by the incessant Dutch demands for their cattle and encroachment on their grazing lands and waterholes. As one group became impoverished and reluctant to trade, another would take its place. The climate of the Cape was well suited to Europeans, and their birth rate was high; whereas in Angola and Mozambique the Portuguese were ravaged by disease, at the Cape it was the indigenes who were decimated by epidemics of smallpox, influenza, and measles brought by Europeans.

By the end of the 18th century, Cape settlers—
called Boers (Dutch *boer*, "farmer")—were far more
numerous than their Portuguese counterparts, largely
because of natural increase. The settlers began to call
themselves "Afrikaners"—Africans. Nevertheless,
class divisions in Cape Town and its environs were
marked. A small group of affluent merchants and
status-conscious company servants lived in Cape
Town; in the neighbouring farming districts of the
southwestern Cape a wealthy gentry used slave labour
to produce wine and wheat for passing ships. Independent small farmers eked out a living on the land, and a
number of landless whites worked for others, generally as supervisors.

SLAVERY AT THE CAPE

The number of slaves increased along with the settler
population, especially in the arable districts. Experi-
ments in the use of indentured European labour were
unsuccessful, and by the mid 18th century about half
the burghers at the Cape owned at least one slave,
though few owned more than 10. Slaves spoke the
creolized Dutch that in the 19th century became Afrikaans. Many adopted Islam, which alarmed the ruling
class. Divided in origin and dispersed geographically,
slaves did not establish a cohesive culture or mount

effective rebellions. Individual acts of defiance were frequent, however, and in the early 19th century there were two small uprisings. Nevertheless, in Cape Town itself slave culture provided the basis for a working-class culture after emancipation.

Mortality rates for slaves were high and birth rates low. Punishments for even minor misdemeanours were fierce, perhaps because adult male slaves greatly outnumbered their owners. Manumission, baptism, and intermarriage rates were also low, although newcomers and poorer burghers married slave women and, more rarely, Khoekhoe women. Cohabitation with indigenous women was more common, especially in frontier districts where there were few white women. The children of these interracial unions, however, took on the unprivileged status of their mothers, so the practice did not affect the racially defined class structure of the society forming at the Cape. By the late 18th century in the Cape most blacks were servants and most Europeans were masters.

The existence of slavery affected the status and opportunities of the dispossessed Khoisan who entered the labour market in increasing numbers from the late 17th century. Although theoretically they were free, compulsion governed the relationship between master and servant, and the legal status of the Khoisan increasingly approximated that of slaves. As they lost their cattle and grazing areas, the Khoisan became virtual serfs on settler farms, although some groups managed to escape beyond colonial borders.

By the end of the 18th century, then, when the British took over, the small Dutch East India Company outpost at the Cape had grown into a sprawling settlement in which some 22,000 whites dominated a labouring class of about 25,000 slaves and approximately as many Khoisan, as well as free blacks and "Prize Negroes"—slaves seized by the Royal Navy and reenslaved in the Cape—in Cape Town and a growing number of Xhosa in the eastern districts.

THE 19TH CENTURY

By the time the Cape changed hands during the Napoleonic Wars, humanitarians were vigorously campaigning against slavery, and in 1807 they succeeded in persuading Britain to abolish the trade. British antislavery ships soon patrolled the western coast of Africa. Ivory became the most important export from west-central Africa, satisfying the growing demand in Europe. The western port of Benguela was the main outlet, and the Ovimbundu and Chokwe, renowned hunters, were the major suppliers. They penetrated deep into south-central Africa, decimating the elephant populations with their firearms.

The more sparse, agricultural Ovambo peoples to the south also were drawn into the ivory trade. Initially trading in salt, copper, and iron from the Etosha Pan region to the north, and supplying hides and ivory to Portuguese traders, the Ovambo largely had been able to avoid the slave trade that ravaged their more populous neighbours. By the mid 19th century the advent of firearms led to a vast increase in the volume of the ivory trade, though the trade collapsed as the elephants were nearly exterminated by the 1880s. By then, traders from Angola, the Cape Colony, and Walvis Bay sought cattle as well as ivory. With the firearms acquired through the trade, Ovambo chiefs built up their power, raiding the pastoral Herero and Nama people in the vast, arid region to their south.

THE CONTINUATION AND EFFECTS OF THE SLAVE TRADE

British antislavery patrols drove the slave trade east, where ivory had been more significant. In the first decades of the 19th century, slave traders for the French sugar plantations in Réunion and Mauritius, who had previously drawn the majority of their slaves from Madagascar, turned their attentions to the coast of Mozambique, while the demand from Cuba and Brazil also escalated. Thus, by the late

1820s Mozambique's slave exports were outstripping those of Angola, with demand from the French islands rivaling that of Brazil by the 1830s. The flow of slaves was augmented by turmoil in the interior of Southern Africa and by slaves captured by the Chikunda soldiers of the Zambezi warlords. By the 1840s rival Zambezi armies were competing to control the trade routes to south-central Africa.

The most important area of slave raiding appears to have been in Malawi and northeastern Zambia, where predatory overlords devastated a wide area from bases in the Congo. The political geography of the region was transformed as people moved into stockaded villages and towns and began to raid one another for captive women to work the fields while the men engaged in warfare. Vast numbers of people, especially women, were torn from their social settings, and earlier divisions based on kin came to matter less than new relationships between patron and client, protector and protected.

It is not possible to compile an exact balance sheet of the devastation caused to Southern Africa by the slave trade, and historians differ in their estimation of the numbers involved and of the extent of the damage inflicted. In the 17th century some 10,000 to 12,000 slaves were exported annually from Luanda. Although this figure includes captives from both north and south

THE "TIME OF TURMOIL"

Given the turbulence caused by slave raiding in east- and west-central Africa, it is tempting to blame this for the unprecedented warfare in Southern Africa in the second and third decades of the 19th century. The Mfecane, or Difaqane ("Crushing"), as this warfare is known, is currently much debated. As yet, however, there seems little evidence for extensive slave trading south of Quelimane until the 1820s, and the slave trade from Inhambane and Delagoa Bay remained paltry until 1823–44; the trade from these ports thus seems more a consequence than a cause of the wars.

Demand for cattle and ivory at Delagoa Bay seems rather more important in the emergence, by the late 18th century, of a number of larger states in the hinterland of Delagoa Bay. Trade gave chiefs new ways of attracting followers, while elephant hunting and cattle raiding honed military organization. In the early 19th century, however, the number of European ships calling at Delagoa Bay appears to have contracted, and this may have increased competition for the cattle and ivory trade. Together with a series of devastating droughts (in 1800–03, 1812, and 1816–18), this competition may better account for the debilitating wars in which the larger northern Nguni chiefdoms in Zululand were embroiled by the second decade of the century; indeed, oral sources attribute the first battles to conflicts over land. These battles occurred even before the rise of the Zulu king Shaka, whom an early historiography holds almost solely responsible for turmoil as far afield as the Cape Colony, Tanzania, and western Zambia.

of the bay, it does not include those smuggled out to escape official taxation.

Neither Portugal's attempt to ban its nationals from slave trading in 1836 nor even the abolition of slavery in Brazil in the 1880s ended slavery in west-central Africa. Local merchants, chiefs, and elders turned to slaves to produce the tropical products demanded by Europeans and to serve as porters for the growing quantities of wax and ivory from the 1840s and '50s and rubber from the 1870s. By 1910 wild rubber accounted for more than three-quarters of Angola's exports by volume. Although the rubber trade was successful in the short term, excessive collection of wild rubber destroyed an irreplaceable natural resource, while new concentrations of population upset the ecological balance of a drought-prone environment.

BRITISH DEVELOPMENT OF THE CAPE COLONY

Britain occupied the Cape Colony at the turn of the 19th century. During the Napoleonic Wars the Cape passed first to the British (1795–1803), then to the Batavian Republic (1803–06), and to the British again in 1806. The main impulse behind Britain's annexation was to protect its sea route to India. However, the British demands that the colony pay for its administration, produce raw materials for the metropole, and provide a market for Britain's manufactures and a home for its unemployed ineluctably drew Britain into defending the colonists, expanding their territory, and transforming the Cape's mercantile economy. The displacement of Dutch East India Company rule by an imperial state in the early stages of its industrial revolution greatly expanded local opportunities for trade and increased demands for labour, just as the slave trade was abolished in the British Empire.

In its constitutional development the Cape Colony followed the pattern set by Britain's other settler colonies in the 19th century. It was initially a crown colony governed by an autocratic governor, whose more extreme powers were modified by the presence in Cape Town of an articulate middle class and by the arrival in 1820 of some 5,000 British settlers. These groups demanded a free press, an independent legal system, the rooting out of corruption, and more representative institutions. After intense political struggle, Cape men were granted representative government in 1853, with a nonracial franchise that included a low property threshold, which, it was hoped, would defuse the discontent of both Afrikaners and the rebellious creolized Khoisan/Coloured population.

CHANGES IN THE STATUS OF AFRICANS

In 1872 the Cape gained full responsible government. The colour-blind franchise was retained but came under increasing attack. As a strategy for incorporating the more prosperous black peasants and artisans, it had been supported by white merchants, professionals, and officials. With the annexation of African territories and the creation of a mass black working class, however, it proved vulnerable, and in 1887 and 1892 the franchise qualifications were changed in order to restrict the number of black voters.

Initially, imperial protection expanded Cape wheat and wine production, while the British did little to alter existing social and property relations. By the mid 1820s, however, imperial attempts to create a "free market" in labour—including the abolition of preferential tariffs and reform in the system of land tenure—had an explosive effect on the class relations of a colony dependent on slaves and serfs. New regulations ensured standards of treatment and established equality before the law for "masters" and "servants." Ordinance 50 of 1828, which ensured Khoisan mobility on the labour market, caused an uproar; in 1834 slaves were finally emancipated. Despite their formal equality before the law, however, newly emancipated slaves received only modest protection, from the handful of mission stations, against exploitative and often brutal conditions. By 1841, largely through "masters and servants" legislation, settlers had reimposed much of their old authority.

Although the underclass received only limited benefits, the British land and labour policies—together with a restructuring of local government—threatened many Afrikaners. Between 1834 and 1838, in a movement known as the Great Trek, parties of Voortrekkers ("Pioneers"), with their families and dependents, departed the Cape Colony. Their exodus was to become the central saga of 20th-century Afrikaner nationalism.

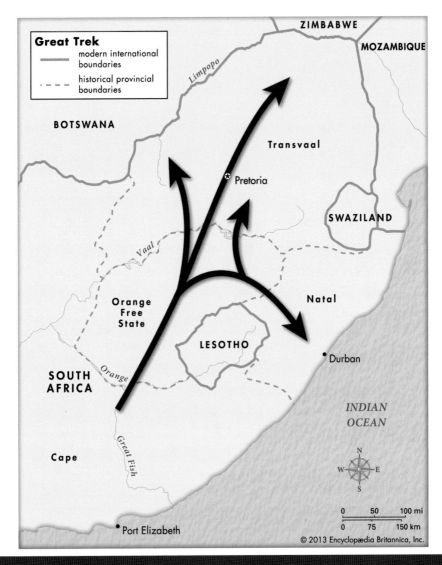

Thousands of Boers made the Great Trek from Cape Colony to the interior of South Africa. They eventually established three separate colonies: Natal, Transvaal, and Orange Free State.

Beyond the confines of the colony, they established separate republics in Natal, the Orange Free State, and the Transvaal, outflanking the Xhosa along the southeast coast, where the British were confronted by a series of interlocking crises.

GROWTH OF MISSIONARY ACTIVITY

From the end of the 18th century, European missionaries were crucial in the transformation of African society at the Cape. With Christianity came Victorian notions of civilization and progress. Progress meant that Africans produced agricultural products for export and entered into the labour market. The first converts in the Cape were the Khoisan, in the east and north, and the Griqua, who by the 1820s had formed a series of independent if schismatic states in the Vaal-Orange confluence. By the late 1820s these states were seen by the missionaries as destined to have a vast "civilizing" influence in the interior. The neighbouring Sotho-Tswana communities were also early sites of missionary activity. Two of the most famous 19th-century Scottish missionaries to Southern Africa, Robert Moffat and David Livingstone, worked among the Tswana. The most notable of the Tswana converts were the Ngwato, under the king Khama III (reigned 1875–1923), who established a

virtual theocracy among his people and was perhaps
the most acclaimed Christian convert of his day,
while in the eastern Cape the Mfengu were in the
forefront of mission activity and peasant enterprise.
In the second half of the 19th century, increasing
numbers of Xhosa also turned to Christianity. In
Zululand and on the Highveld the missionaries both
preceded and paved the way for white settlers and
were sometimes their fiercest critics.

Initially Christianity tended to advance most
rapidly among the disaffected and dispossessed, and
especially among women, with those who depended
on the slave trade less enthusiastic. It was usually
only after a major disaster undermined their belief
systems that considerable numbers of men turned
to the new religion. By inculcating individualism
and encouraging the stratification that was to lead
so many of their converts onto the colonial labour
markets, the missionaries attacked much that was
central to African society and developed an ideology
to accompany colonial subordination.

The first European missionaries to south-central
Africa, inspired by Livingstone, set up their Universities Mission in 1861. Although this mission ended
in tragedy and failure, after Livingstone's death in
1873 other missionaries followed. In 1875 the Free
Church of Scotland established the Livingstonia

Mission in his memory, while the established Church of Scotland began work among the Yao at Blantyre the following year. From Lake Nyasa the Scottish missions spread inland to northeastern Zambia and were followed by a large number of representatives of other Christian denominations in the last decades of the century. By the last quarter of the 19th century, European missionaries and African evangelists of almost every denomination were working among the peoples of Southern Africa, eroding chiefly authority and inculcating the new values and practices of the colonial world but also bringing new modes of resistance and educating many Christian Africans who later became outspoken critics of colonialism.

THE EXPANSION OF WHITE SETTLEMENT

If the expansion of white settlement under the British led to a vast expropriation of African land and labour, it also led to a rapid expansion of unequal trading relations. Black-white exchange existed in the frontier zone from the early 18th century. British traders soon crossed colonial frontiers and were at Shaka's court by the early 1820s. They exchanged African cattle and crops for beads and brandy and on occasion may have purchased slaves, although even settlers well beyond colonial boundaries now disguised this as "apprenticeship" and "indenture." The establishment of republics throughout the 19th century meant that black Africans continued to lose land and ultimately their independence to white-dominated governments.

The Boers established a republic in Natal, but, in 1843, the British, anxious to control the sea route to India, fearful of trekker negotiations with foreign powers, and concerned that trekker raids would spread to the eastern frontier, annexed the region, leaving the Zulu kingdom north of the Tugela River independent until its disintegration in the civil wars that followed its defeat by the British army in 1879. For most of the 19th century, British Natal was surrounded by powerful African states and was heavily outnumbered by Africans within the colony. Racial practices in Natal—including the reservation of lands for African communal occupation, recognition of tribal authorities, codification of customary law, and control over urbanization through labour registration and influx control—were born out of the colony's weakness and provided precedents for 20th-century segregationist policies.

With the British annexation of Natal, most of the Voortrekkers rejoined their compatriots on the Highveld, where separate communities had been established in Transorangia (the region across the Orange River) and the western and northeastern Transvaal. On the Highveld the Voortrekkers entered a vibrant and complex African world. To ensconce themselves in the interior, they fought major wars and established a series of accommodations with those Africans whom they were unable to conquer. Compared with the British colonies, the racially exclusive republics between the Vaal, Hartz, and Limpopo rivers were weak members of the world economy, dependent on cattle ranching and hunting. Bitterly divided politically and ecclesiastically, these republics were unified in 1860 as the South African Republic, annexed as the British colony of the Transvaal between 1877 and 1881, and reconquered as the Transvaal during the South African War (1899–1902).

Farther south, in Transorangia, a far greater proportion of the small settler community was tied to Cape and British markets through wool production. Of a population in 1875 of some 125,000, only the 26,000 whites had citizenship, but many European observers considered the Orange Free State, with its parliament and written constitution, a model republic. Despite the Dutch ancestry of the majority of the settlers, English was the language of commerce and education into the 20th century. Because of its location, there was continued conflict with several native African peoples.

MINERALS AND THE SCRAMBLE FOR SOUTHERN AFRICA

From the 1860s it was known that there was gold in the interior of Southern Africa. In 1867 diamonds were discovered at Kimberley in Griqualand West to the north of the Cape Colony, followed shortly thereafter by discoveries of outcrop (surface) gold in the Transvaal and deep seams of gold on the Witwatersrand in 1886. The conjuncture of speculation in mining futures and land, the imposition of colonial or company rule, and an industrial revolution based on mineral extraction meant that the last third of the 19th century was one of the most traumatic in the history of the region. The language of racial domination, though hardly new, was now buttressed by social Darwinism and was particularly well suited to an era of intensified land and labour exploitation.

The mineral discoveries led to dramatic economic development. Roads, railways, and harbours were built. New coal mines were exploited. Manufacturing, though in its infancy, responded to the new markets, while the creation of an internal market for food was crucial in the commercialization of agriculture and the spread of African cash crop production. Land prices soared, and the demand for labour became insatiable. A working class—consisting of both whites and blacks—was created out of the preindustrial societies. Colonial conquest subjugated the remaining independent African societies and destroyed the bargaining power of black workers.

THE DIAMOND INDUSTRY

Although most scholarly attention has focused on the gold mines, it was the diamond industry that pioneered many of the characteristics of Southern Africa's labour control policies. People from all over the world came to Griqualand West to seek their fortune; between 1871 and 1875 more than 50,000 Africans from all over the subcontinent came each year, many of them lured by the prospect of purchasing firearms. Within a few years there was hardly an African chiefdom, from the Transkei to the Limpopo, that was not armed with guns. Combined with the progressive encroachment on African lands and the intensifying demand for their labour, the rearming of Africans was a major source of the instability of these years.

Initially, claims on the diamond fields were limited, technology was primitive, and small-scale black diggers could compete with whites. In the mid 1870s, however, chaotic production conditions, a flooded world diamond market, and labour shortages made the transition to larger units of production necessary. Joint-stock companies were created, bringing international capital and a transformation of mining technology. By 1888 the thousands of claims of the previous decade had been monopolized by the De Beers Mining Company. For black and white workers the establishment of the De Beers monopoly was of immense significance. African migrant workers were now more rigorously controlled by pass laws, which limited their mobility, and by confinement to compounds for the duration of their work contracts. Many white miners lost their jobs or became overseers, and wages for all workers were sharply reduced.

THE DISCOVERY OF GOLD

With the discovery of the Witwatersrand, attention switched from Kimberley to the South African Republic, which was quickly transformed from a ramshackle and bankrupt agrarian outpost to the most important state in the subcontinent. The coastal colonies competed to control the lucrative Witwatersrand trade, and immigration mounted: in 1870 the total white population of Southern Africa was probably less than 250,000; by 1891 it had increased to more than 600,000; and by 1904 it was more than 1,000,000. When local capital proved inadequate, funds flowed in from Britain, Germany, and France. From the late 1880s gold outstripped diamonds as the region's most important export, and by 1898 the Witwatersrand produced about one-fifth of world gold output.

In 1889 the Chamber of Mines, an organization of mine owners, was formed to drive down the costs of production. This became even more important once deep-level mines were opened in the mid 1890s, because development costs were high, the ore low-grade, and the price of gold controlled. Skilled, unionized white workers from the mining frontiers of the world were able to protect their high wages, while the chamber formed two major recruiting organizations, the Witwatersrand Native Labour Association (Wenela) and the Native Recruiting Corporation, to extend, monopolize, and control the black labour supply throughout the subcontinent.

Throughout the region it was usually young men who were the first migrants, often sent by homestead heads, who tried to control their movement and their wages, or by chiefs who received a recruitment fee or a portion of the labourer's wages in tribute. For many young men a period of labour migration could bring independent access to bridewealth. Although the process had its roots in the migration of Africans to colonial labour markets earlier in the century, migrant labour expanded after the mineral discoveries and had profound ramifications for the control of senior men over juniors and colonial administrators over taxpayers. Chiefs thus became increasingly anxious over their lack of control over young men and women and struck alliances with colonial administrators and recruiting agents to secure the return of migrants.

THE ANNEXATION OF SOUTHERN AFRICA

The first move in the scramble for Southern Africa came with renewed assertions of British supremacy in the interior. After much dispute, Britain annexed Griqualand West as a crown colony in 1871, transferring it to the Cape Colony in 1881. The multiple crises following the diamond discoveries led during the 1870s to failed imperial schemes to confederate the Southern African territories, but imperial wars between 1878 and 1884 effectively ended the independence of the major African kingdoms. Of these conquests the best-known was the war in 1879 against the Zulu, which included a spectacular defeat of the British army at Isandhlwana.

The mineral discoveries whetted German imperial ambitions, and in 1884 Germany annexed the vast, sparsely populated territory of South West Africa (now Namibia). The annexation challenged British hegemony in the region, raised fears of a German-Transvaal alliance, and accelerated the scramble for Southern Africa. The possibilities of mineral wealth in the interior also revived Portugal's dream of uniting its African colonies. Portugal received short shrift from the other powers, however. At the Berlin West Africa Conference of 1884–85, Portugal secured the Cabinda exclave and a portion of the left bank of the Congo River on the Atlantic coast—considerably less than it claimed—and in 1886 the Kunene-Okavango region went to Germany. Portugal gained even less in Mozambique, which remained a narrow coastal corridor.

With the discovery of gold, the remaining independent African polities south of the Limpopo were conquered and annexed, and both within and beyond colonial frontiers concessionaires were spurred by prospects of further discoveries and the availability of speculative capital. The Limpopo constituted no barrier, and between 1889 and 1895 all the African territories south of the Congo territory were annexed. In south-central Africa the British competed with the South African Republic, Portugal, Germany, and Belgium, while in east-central Africa, to the west and south of Lake Nyasa, the thrust from the south encountered the less powerful but still significant antislavery missionary and trading frontier from the east.

For many of the peoples of the subcontinent, the first phase of colonialism may have been overshadowed by the series of disasters that struck rural society in the mid 1890s, including locusts, drought, smallpox and other diseases, and a disastrous rinderpest epidemic that decimated African cattle holdings in 1896–97. Whereas before the colonial period such natural disasters would have killed large numbers in the short term but probably would have had little long-term consequence, the disasters of the 1890s drew considerable numbers of Africans into dependence on colonial labour markets for the first time and thus permanently changed the structure of African society.

From the 1860s it was known that there were "ancient gold workings" beyond the Limpopo. In 1887–88 the high commissioner at the Cape declared the region a British sphere of interest. It was at this point that Cecil John Rhodes entered the arena.

CECIL RHODES IN SOUTHERN AFRICA

The story of how Rhodes came to South Africa to repair his frail health and stayed to become a millionaire on the diamond fields before he was 30 is legendary. In 1880 he entered the Cape parliament, and in the 1880s he played a key role in securing the British annexation of the Tswana kingdoms that straddled the road to the interior. One of the leading mine owners in Kimberley, by 1888 he had bought out his rivals and created the De Beers consortium. In 1890, when he became the Cape's prime minister, he was the most powerful man in Southern Africa.

Rhodes hoped to find in south-central Africa a "second Rand" to outflank the South African Republic. In 1888 his agents secured exclusive mining rights from Lobengula for Rhodes's British South Africa Company (BSAC), which was granted a royal charter by the British government to exploit and extend administrative control over a vast area of south-central and Southern Africa. Across the Zambezi, where the British were anxious to preempt European rivals, Rhodes engaged the newly appointed British consul for Malawi

Photo : Bassano, Old Bond Street, W.

MR. CECIL RHODES.

The financier, statesman, and empire builder Cecil Rhodes became the prime minister of Cape Colony and the organizer of the massive diamond-mining company De Beers Consolidated Mines, Ltd.

and Mozambique, Harry Johnston, to establish his company's claims.

A flurry of treaty making in 1888–89 left the BSAC with land and mineral concessions throughout present-day Malawi and Zambia. Despite the dubious legality of the treaties, the chiefs agreed to accept British jurisdiction over non-Africans in their domains and over external relations. In the European chancellories, where the frontiers of Africa were being decided, the treaties played an important role in negotiations. In 1890–91 British, Portuguese, and German conventions established the frontiers of many of the modern states of Southern Africa.

For Britain the BSAC's great advantage was its promise to make British occupation effective against contending European powers and to bring capitalist development at minimum cost. In 1890 Rhodes sent a "Pioneer Column," consisting of 200 white settlers and 150 blacks, backed by 500 police, into Mashonaland; the real goal was the Ndebele kingdom, which was conquered in a deliberately provoked war in 1893. Although Matabeleland's conquest brought an anticipated boom in BSAC shares, by the end of 1894 it was clear that there was no "second Rand" in south-central Africa and that the future lay with the new deep-level mines coming into operation farther south.

EXPROPRIATION OF AFRICAN LAND

As their hopes of discovering gold waned, settlers and the BSAC began expropriating African land, labor, and cattle. Settlers who participated in the war were granted lavish farms and mineral claims, both of which soon passed to speculative syndicates. A land commission perfunctorily set aside two reserves for the Ndebele on poor soils. In 1896 the Ndebele rose in revolt and were joined by a number of eastern Shona polities. Only the arrival of imperial troops and the collaboration of other Shona groups saved the company state. The uprising led the British to intervene directly in BSAC affairs by appointing a resident commissioner in Bulawayo responsible to the imperial high commissioner in Cape Town.

These events left few resources for occupation north of the Zambezi until the late 1890s. Opposition from missionaries and the African Lakes Company ensured that the region around Lake Nyasa and the Shire River valley was separated from the BSAC sphere; it was declared the British Central African Protectorate in 1891, with Johnston as commissioner. Even before Johnston's arrival the British had been embroiled in open warfare with Arab slave traders, and during the early years of the protectorate Johnston engaged in a spate of wars against the Swahili and Yao slave and ivory traders, who feared the loss of their livelihood. Given the fragmentation and social divisions of the region, he found little difficulty in implementing a policy of divide and rule. Johnston's antislavery wars had the advantage of releasing labour for European employers. Wary of creating a landless proletariat, Johnston, like Rhodes, nevertheless believed that the protectorate's future development should be based on the marriage of white enterprise and black labour, assisted by Asian middlemen.

West of the protectorate, Africans were drawn more gradually under colonial rule, despite pleas from the Lozi king Lewanika that the British provide technical and financial assistance in exchange for mineral concessions, as promised in an 1890 treaty. Despite Lewanika's "protected" status, over the next decade the powers of the king and the aristocracy were whittled away. British insistence on the abolition of serfdom and slavery in 1906 undermined the cultivation of the floodplain on which Lozi agriculture depended, and Lewanika's hopes to control the modernization of his state were not fulfilled. Bulozi became a protectorate within a protectorate, tied to the Southern African political economy.

In northeastern Zambia, the process of imposing colonial rule was swifter and less violent than it had been to the south or east. The natural disasters of the 1890s diminished the ability of the more powerful groups to resist, while weaker peoples at first welcomed the end of Bemba, Ngoni, and Swahili exactions. A lack of resources spared the region major confrontations with colonialism (by contrast, among the Ngoni led by Mpeseni, where gold was believed to exist, the onslaught was as dramatic as in Zimbabwe and the expropriation as brutal). Nevertheless, attempts to impose closer settlement, interfere with local agricultural techniques, and extract forced labour combined with natural disasters to produce extremely high morbidity and mortality rates in the early years of company rule.

THE PORTUGUESE

For much of the 19th century, Portuguese colonists in Angola and Mozambique were fewer in number and weaker in authority than those in the interior of South Africa. At the beginning of the century, fewer than 1,000 settlers in each colony huddled on a number of estates around inland forts, along the Bengo and Dande rivers in Angola, and along the lower Zambezi in Mozambique. Most intermarried with local peoples and were independent of Portugal. The metropolitan Portuguese were unable to control either the coastal trade or the activities of the merchants and warlords in the hinterland, who often acted in their name. Despite a mythology that held that the Portuguese, unlike the northern Europeans,

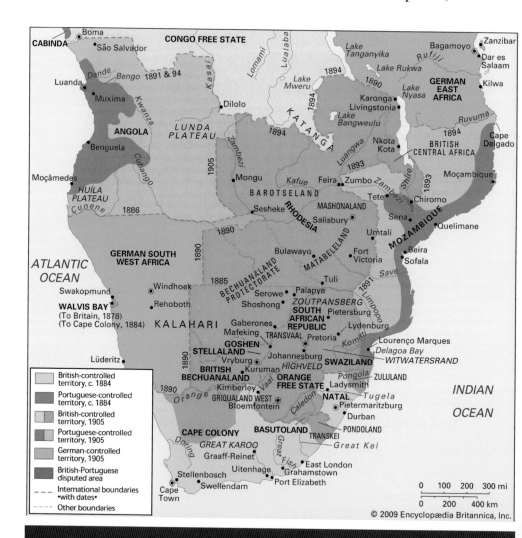

This map shows the European penetration into Southern Africa in the late 19th and early 20th centuries. As you can see, the territory under European control expanded greatly between 1884 and 1905.

did not differentiate according to race, from early times it is clear that whites had superior status and prestige—if not always greater power—in Angola and Mozambique.

From the mid 19th century, Portuguese capital began to enter the colony. The Portuguese made land grants in the Luanda hinterland, and planters experimented with raising coffee, cotton, cacao, and sugarcane, using the slaves who could no longer be exported. In the absence of an adequate administration or communications network, the plantations in Angola were never highly successful. The appropriation of African land for plantations was resisted, and Portuguese attempts to expand their colonial nucleus led to a series of wars with African peoples, followed by famine and epidemics. The instability of the last decades of the 19th century paved the way for the colonial period that followed.

Portuguese attempts to develop Mozambique met with even less success, given the lack of investment and prevailing disorder, as escaped slaves, soldiers, and porters formed bandit bands in broken country and attacked Portuguese settlements and African villages. In many areas domestic slavery underpinned the migration of young men to the labour markets of the south by the 1850s. Liberal governments in Portugal from mid century were anxious to outlaw the feudal aspects of the *prazo* system but were unsuccessful, despite four military campaigns and a declaration in 1880 that the *prazos* were crown property

Until the 1890s the Portuguese had little authority beyond their coastal enclaves. The only bright spot in their fortunes in southeastern Africa was the growing prosperity of Delagoa Bay, as trade with the Transvaal increased. In 1875 Portuguese rights to Delagoa Bay were recognized internationally. With the discovery of gold in the South African Republic, the bay acquired a new importance as its closest outlet, and in 1888 Lourenço Marques became the capital of Mozambique.

Although Portugal failed in its major territorial ambitions in the late 19th century, it nonetheless acquired about 800,000 square miles (2,000,000 square km) of African territory, of which it controlled about one-tenth. In both Portuguese territories "pacification" became a sine qua non of economic development, and there were military campaigns or police actions in almost every year between 1875 and 1924, a measure of Portugal's weakness as a colonial power. The greatest resistance came from those people with the longest experience of Portuguese rule and with the necessary firearms. In Angola the major campaigns were against the Kongo, Mbundu, and

Ovambo peoples; in Mozambique against peoples of the Zambezi valley, the Islamized Makua and Yao, and the Gaza kingdom, which was finally defeated in 1895.

The majority of Portuguese troops in both territories were black, a situation that turned every campaign into a potential civil war. Fragmentation of political authority, resistance of traditional elites threatened by colonial rule, and the precipitate introduction of taxes and forced labour policies also made resistance in the Portuguese colonies the most prolonged in early 20th-century Africa.

Colonial markets were of particular importance to Portugal, and tariff barriers were erected to protect its manufactures. Starved of capital and racked by financial crises, Portugal planned to develop the colonies by attracting immigration and foreign capital and by fostering plantation agriculture. In Mozambique, however, local employers could not compete with the Witwatersrand. Since the 1850s, Mozambican migrants had traveled to the farms and sugar plantations of South Africa, while by the 1870s sterling had begun to replace cattle and hoes as bridewealth. By 1897 more than half the mine workers on the Rand came from Mozambique, while thousands worked on South African farms.

GERMANS IN SOUTH WEST AFRICA

The Germans were the last imperial power to arrive in Africa. Their annexation and control of South West Africa was eased by the intense cleavages that had opened up between the local Nama and the Herero chiefdoms, a result of their increasing involvement in the world economy during the 19th century.

Throughout the 19th century, displaced communities of Khoekhoe and Oorlams from the Cape had made their way into South West Africa, competing for the sparse water and grazing land. At first they settled peacefully on land granted them by the local populace, some of them establishing mission communities. The advent in the 1830s of the Oorlam chief Jonker Afrikaner and his well-armed followers significantly altered the regional balance of power. Responding to an appeal from the Nama, who were being driven from their grazing lands by Herero expansion, Afrikaner settled at Windhoek. By gaining control over the all-important trade routes from Walvis Bay and the Cape Colony, he ensured, until his death in 1861, Nama dominance over the Herero. Wars between the Nama and Herero were exacerbated from the mid 19th century by the increasing cattle and ivory trade and the availability of firearms; apart from a breathing space between 1870 and 1880, the Nama-Herero wars continued from 1863 to 1892.

Initially Germany hoped to exploit the territory through a concession company, but it could not raise sufficient capital. The government was increasingly forced to intervene in local affairs, especially when settlers appropriated Herero cattle and grazing lands. The most formidable opponent of the Germans was Hendrik Witbooi, a Nama chief who tried unsuccessfully to unite the Herero and Nama against the Germans. After a lengthy guerrilla war, he was defeated in 1894.

The rinderpest epidemic, the alienation of the better-watered highlands, unfair trading practices, and increasing indebtedness led to an uprising by the Nama and Herero peoples in 1904–07. They were crushed in a genocidal campaign: the Herero population fell from about 70,000 to about 16,000, with many dying in the desert while attempting to escape. The Nama were reduced by two-fifths. The handful of settlers had to turn for labour to the Cape Colony and Ovamboland, which was formally brought under colonial rule only when the South Africans took over South West Africa during World War I.

THE SOUTH AFRICAN WAR

If the Nama-Herero wars were among the most savage in colonial Africa, an equally bitter, costly colonial war was fought by Britain against the Afrikaner South African Republic. The reasons for the South African (or Anglo-Boer) War (1899–1902) remain controversial: some historians portray it in personal terms, the result of clashes between the president of the South African Republic, Paul Kruger, and the representatives of British imperialism, Rhodes and the high commissioner, Sir Alfred Milner; some argue that the British feared that the regional dominance of the South African Republic would open the way for German intervention in the subcontinent and endanger the sea route to India; others believe that the struggle was for supremacy over the richest gold mines in the world and the need to establish a state in the Transvaal that would fulfill the demands of the deep-level mine owners.

Even before the war, the South African Republic's inability to create and coerce a labour force was irksome to the deep-level mine owners, with their huge demand for labour and tight working costs. The liquor, railway, and dynamite policies of the South African Republic also angered the mine owners. Taking advantage of the fomented clamour of British immigrants over their lack of voting rights and secretly backed by the British colonial secretary Joseph Chamberlain, Rhodes plotted the armed overthrow of the republic by his lieutenant Leander Starr Jameson.

The Jameson Raid in December 1895 was a complete fiasco. There was no internal uprising, and the raiders were soon arrested. Rhodes was forced to resign from the premiership of the Cape Colony, and the alliance he had carefully constructed between English and Afrikaners in the Cape was destroyed. Previously loyal to the empire, Cape Afrikaners now backed Kruger against the British, as did their fellows in the Orange Free State. Nascent pan-South African Afrikaner nationalism received a push. Milner's determination to assert British supremacy exacerbated matters, and in 1899 a rearmed South African Republic issued an ultimatum to the British that amounted to a declaration of war. Over the next three and a half years, nearly 500,000 British troops were deployed against an Afrikaner force of 60,000 to 65,000, at great cost to the British taxpayers. Some 6,000 British soldiers died in action and another 16,000 of infectious diseases. The Afrikaners lost some 14,000 in action and 26,000 in concentration camps. The camps powerfully inflamed 20th-century Afrikaner nationalism. Although the total number of African dead is unrecorded, according to low official estimates, more than 100,000 were forced into camps and at least 13,000 died there. In the end, Britain's greater resources wore the Afrikaners down; their leaders were forced to sue for peace, and a treaty was signed on May 31, 1902.

Even before the war ended, Milner had begun to "reconstruct" the vanquished Afrikaner republics; the most serious grievances of the mine magnates

This photograph shows Boer troops lining up in battle during the South African War. The conflict is also known as the Anglo-Boer War, the Boer War, and the Second Boer War.

were removed, and an efficient bureaucracy was established. The smooth functioning of the mining industry was crucial both politically and economically. An acute shortage of unskilled African labour was resolved by the importation of 60,000 Chinese, despite the bitter opposition of white workers, and ambitious schemes were hatched to reduce the cost of both black and white labour.

Africans were effectively disarmed and systematically taxed for the first time, and the pass laws were made more efficient. These changes also benefited white farmers, who were assisted in a variety of ways by the state. By 1906–07 the British were sufficiently confident of the new order they had established to grant self-governing institutions to male whites in the conquered territories, and in 1910, under the South Africa Act passed by the British Parliament in 1909, the four South African colonies of Transvaal, Natal, Orange Free State, and the Cape were unified as provinces of the Union of South Africa. Although much British propaganda before and during the South African War had been concerned with the political rights of British subjects regardless of colour, outside the Cape province blacks remained excluded from citizenship.

SOUTHERN AFRICA IN THE EARLY 20TH CENTURY

By the beginning of the 20th century the subcontinent was under European rule, and its disparate societies were increasingly meshed into a single political economy. The annexation of African territories meant the establishment of new states, and colonial rule was given perceptible effect by policemen and soldiers, administrators, tax collectors, traders, prospectors, and labour recruiters. Railroads connected the coast with the interior, opening up new markets and releasing new sources of labour. New boundaries were drawn that lasted beyond the colonial period, and the Zambezi became the frontier between the settler south and the "tropical dependencies" of East and Central Africa, although Nyasaland (Malawi) and Northern Rhodesia (Zambia) occupied a middle ground.

The exploitation of minerals, the capitalization of settler agriculture, and the establishment of manufacturing industries drew Africans into the world economy as workers and peasants, transforming class structures and political alignments and shifting the division of labour between men and women. Previously male occupations, such as hunting and warfare, declined. Indigenous production of nonagricultural commodities from cotton to iron suffered from the competition of cheap, mass-produced imports. The costs of colonialism were unequally distributed. In the areas of white colonization, the BSAC and the colonial powers supported the settlers. Elsewhere African ruling elites were able to strike compromises with their new overlords. On the reserves and protectorates of Southern Africa, chiefs and hereditary headmen still controlled their followings, although their authority was eroded as they became appointees of the colonial authorities. Again the process varied from area to area. Whereas colonial authorities initially attempted to destroy the overarching powers of the African kings and paramounts, who had led the military resistance to colonialism and symbolized the cohesion of their people, the role of intermediate chiefs in providing a cheap administrative infrastructure was soon recognized.

GROWTH OF RACISM

Some blacks and whites, particularly those who had been educated or had prior experience, were able to take advantage of economic opportunities developing in new towns and markets. Yet, for the growing numbers of mission-educated Africans and Coloured and for Indian communities in Southern Africa, the period was probably one of regression rather than advance. European racist ideology replaced an older tradition in the Cape of social dominance through economic control. Strident settler demands for urban segregation classified even wealthy Indian merchants as "uncivilized natives." Indian immigration into all the South African colonies was restricted, and in Natal a number of anti-Indian discriminatory measures followed the grant of responsible government in 1893. In the Cape, institutions became increasingly segregated. While the establishment of new colonial states contributed to the creation of new forms of national consciousness, black hopes of inclusion in the wider society were dashed by the South Africa Act of 1909 and by the establishment of settler-only representative institutions elsewhere. White racism, though still embryonic outside South Africa, fueled African nationalism throughout the region.

Racially discriminatory policies were prompted by settlers' fears of competition from blacks and the growth of black class consciousness; they were given an intellectual underpinning by anthropologists and administrators fearful of rapid social change. The Portuguese espoused policies of African assimilation, yet obstacles to progress for the Afro-Portuguese and acculturated African elite were more rigidly enforced in the 20th century than they had been in the 19th. Before 1945 the ideology of segregation was espoused by virtually all the governments of the region and by most whites regardless of political persuasion. Segregation had different meanings for different groups, but throughout Southern Africa it unified contradictory white interests under a single political slogan, buttressed white power and protected white workers and farmers, and attempted to defuse black militancy at a time of urbanization and social change. For blacks segregation meant exclusion from citizenship; incorporation into a restricted and racially segmented labour market based on the use of migrant labour; government control of movement, urban residence, and trade union organization; the consolidation of the authority of the chiefs; and a recognition or invention of black ethnic identity in the African reserves.

SOUTH AFRICA'S ATTEMPTS AT EXPANSION

South Africa was at the centre of Britain's Southern Africa policies. Nevertheless, until the 1930s the Union was poor, divided, and dominated by international capital. White settlers were Britain's closest allies. Although it overpowered its immediate neighbours, South Africa's expansionist ambitions in the region were largely blocked.

BASUTOLAND, BECHUANALAND, AND SWAZILAND

In 1910 the Union wished to incorporate Basutoland (now Lesotho), Bechuanaland (now Botswana), and Swaziland—three landlocked territories that, through a variety of historical accidents, had remained outside South African control. African and humanitarian opposition and Britain's desire for a foothold in the region prevented this incorporation, and the territories remained British protectorates. Until the mid 20th century, however, both Britain and South Africa assumed that the territories would ultimately become part of South Africa.

Although this did not happen, Basutoland, Bechuanaland, and Swaziland were locked into South Africa's economy. All three territories, which had been grain and cattle exporters at the turn of the century, became increasingly dependent on the South African labour market, especially after South Africa implemented protectionist measures for white farmers. Administrators were often South African, and the form of indirect rule they practiced strengthened the authority of conservative chiefs, leaving little room for political progress. This dual administration, as well as the dependent economies of the territories, were severely castigated by the Pim Commission of 1934–35, but, despite modest reforms, the territories remained poor and neglected.

OVAMBOLAND

The Union was more successful in acquiring the vast colony of South West Africa, which it conquered from the Germans during World War I. Despite a League of Nations mandate that South West Africa be administered as a "sacred trust" for its indigenous inhabitants, South Africa's concern was to foster mining, which dominated the economy, and to subsidize poor Afrikaner settlement in what was known as the "Police Zone." In 1917 Ovamboland, in the north, was annexed; better-watered and therefore more densely populated, Ovamboland had long been able to resist dispossession. During the interwar years South Africa was able to defy the many resolutions passed by the League of Nations urging African social and educational advancement, and the country continued to defy them even when the South African mandate was withdrawn by the United Nations in 1946.

RHODESIA

South Africa also had designs on Southern Rhodesia. However, when the British South Africa Company relinquished control of Southern Rhodesia in 1922, the predominantly British settlers opted for self-government under British rule, and the territory became a self-governing colony the following year. While British subjects of all races were enfranchised, high property qualifications excluded from voting the vast majority of Africans, who formed 95 percent of the population, and an essentially white parliament controlled all the colony's affairs. An imperial veto over discriminatory legislation was rarely exercised. Between the 1920s and '50s the governing party generally remained closely allied to the small group of mining companies that controlled the economy, while the opposition usually represented white farming and working-class interests.

Self-government for the handful of whites was clearly impossible in Nyasaland and Northern Rhodesia, although in both colonies settlers were given some representation on the Legislative Councils that were established in Nyasaland in 1907 and in Northern Rhodesia in 1924. With the discovery of copper, the white population in Northern Rhodesia increased, but whites never achieved a political dominance comparable to that of their compatriots farther south.

Although copper mining was interrupted by the worldwide depression of the 1930s, by the eve of World War II Northern Rhodesia was a major producer, with nearly nine-tenths of its export earnings coming from copper. In 1939 there were about 13,000 whites in the territory. In Nyasaland the BSAC hoped settlers would develop the territory, but white immigration was restricted by Nyasaland's sluggish economic prospects. In both territories racially discriminatory policies protected the interests of white settlers over those of blacks in every sphere. Nevertheless, the small numbers of whites and British proclamations of the paramountcy of African interests, however limited in practice, differentiated these territories from those farther south.

SETTLERS IN MOZAMBIQUE AND ANGOLA

In Mozambique and Angola, too, settler numbers remained small, despite Portugal's schemes to encourage colonial immigration. Before World War I, colonists consisted mainly of illiterate and unskilled peasants. Power remained in the hands of the governor-general, the highest colonial representative of the Portuguese government. In Angola the collapse of rubber prices in 1913 added to settler problems, and many went bankrupt; in northern Mozambique, campaigns against the Germans during World War I led to famine, forced labour, and high mortality from combat and disease. After the war, however, the colonies attracted new settlers as their economies recovered on the strength of increasing world prices for tropical products. In Angola, diamond production in the northwest was an additional stimulus for settlement.

The republican period in Portugal (1910–26) was accompanied by a flurry of activity among settler political groups, some of them in alliance with the Afro-Portuguese and members of the Creole elite angered by bureaucratic inefficiency and corruption. With the inauguration of Portugal's authoritarian "New State" in the early 1930s under António Salazar, however, immigration schemes were dropped and strict vigilance was exercised over all political and economic activity in the colonies. Consultative institutions disappeared, and grand imperial rhetoric accompanied a return to protectionism, fostering Portugal's needs for cheap raw materials and a closed market.

CLASS AND ETHNIC TENSIONS AMONG WHITE SETTLERS

In the new dispensation, whites, with state assistance, controlled private property and the means of production, while Africans were seen solely as labour. In South Africa after 1912 and the British colony of Southern Rhodesia after 1923, settlers controlled the police and armed forces; elsewhere Africans manned the police and armies of the colonial state, although imperial troops remained the ultimate authority.

Settlers everywhere were united in their determination to assert white supremacy but were divided by class and ethnicity. Particularly in South Africa, South West Africa, and Southern Rhodesia, political struggles among whites were often bitter. In South West Africa, German and Afrikaner settlers lived in uneasy tension, which increased in the 1930s when pro-Nazi demonstrations advocating a German takeover of the colony were common. In the Rhodesias, too, there was antagonism between British settlers and Afrikaners who made their way to the territory in the early years of the 20th century, as well as conflicts between the BSAC and white workers and farmers.

These political struggles were most intense in South Africa, which had the most developed economy, the largest and most diverse population (African, Indian, Coloured, and white), and the most acute class and ethnic differences. In the early 20th century "racial conflict" referred to the conflict between settlers of British origin and Afrikaners. Class warfare between white workers and the mine magnates on the Rand was fierce until the 1920s. The years after the creation of the Union were turbulent, with a civil war between Afrikaners when South Africa joined the British side in World War I. A series of mine strikes culminated in 1922 when recently proletarianized Afrikaners, still dreaming of restoring their republic, and members of the newly formed Communist Party of South Africa joined ranks. A five-day battle between white workers and troops on the Witwatersrand ended with 230 dead and the defeat of the workers after martial law was declared; the ringleaders were later hanged.

The South Africa Act of 1909 enfranchised white adult males, but, except for a diminishing proportion of black male property holders in the Cape, neither blacks nor women were enfranchised. Although white women received the vote in 1930, in 1936 Cape African men were removed from the common voters roll, and in 1956 the Coloured voters of the

Cape were similarly disenfranchised. White men effectively were given control over the majority of blacks, and they retained this control until the first democratic, nonracial election in South Africa in April 1994.

LAND, LABOUR, AND TAXATION

Everywhere in early 20th-century Southern Africa the priority of administrations was for labour and revenue, and an extensive tax system was developed to address both needs. Where land shortages did not suffice to push Africans into the labour market, taxation frequently did. In many areas the colonial state was weak, and colonial administrators feared rousing widespread resistance; efforts to collect taxes were often followed by flogging, hut burning, and the confiscation of crops or cattle. Violence was often most intense where administrations were weakest. In areas that had been under colonial rule for more extended periods, legislation forced Africans who had not already been dispossessed of their land into the labour market.

As long as Africans had access to land, however, they had some bargaining power. Money for taxes could be earned by increasing crop production or by selling cattle. In many areas women did most of the farming, and young men worked periodically on white farms and in mines to earn money for cattle, fertilizer, seed, and plows. In the long run, however, Africans became locked into the money economy, and land shortage and indebtedness brought ever-increasing numbers into the labour market.

WHITE AGRICULTURE AND AFRICAN RESERVES

At the beginning of the 20th century the vast majority of Africans in the subcontinent still lived by farming, though in many areas they had become rent- or labour-paying tenants and sharecroppers on land claimed by settlers, syndicates, and speculators. During the 20th century these various forms of tenancy were transformed into wage labour, as white farms became increasingly capitalized.

Throughout the subcontinent, lands were reserved for sole African occupation by administrations fearful that total dispossession would lead to widespread African resistance. In South Africa, mining capitalists also came to see the utility of the reserves in subsidizing cheap labour: the limited agricultural production of the reserves supported the families of migrants, who could then be paid as single workers. On the other hand, white farmers wanted to take over the African reserves for their own use, eliminate competition from African producers, and reduce the employment status of Africans from tenancy to labour service. The Native Lands Act of 1913 and supplementary legislation in 1936 harmonized these conflicting interests, setting aside about one-eighth of South African land for the some 4,000,000 Africans, while reserving the rest for about 1,250,000 whites.

In Swaziland the 3,000 whites who had gained land as temporary concessions from the king in the late 19th century retained virtually two-thirds of the total in land settlements in 1908 and 1915. In response the Swazi royal family gained much popular support by establishing a national fund to repurchase the alienated lands, and by 1968 it had acquired almost half of the total. Basutoland, which had been deprived of its most fertile lands in the 19th century, was a de facto reserve, although, as in Bechuanaland, land remaining in African hands was inalienable.

In Southern Rhodesia, too, where the BSAC developed commercial farming to attract immigrants and raise revenue, even the limited African reserves that had been set aside at imperial insistence were a subject of constant contention. The crucial legislation was the Land Apportionment Act of 1930, which barred African landownership outside the reserves, except in a special freehold purchase area set aside for "progressive farmers." The best land was allocated to whites; less than one-third went to Africans, while about one-fifth remained unassigned. From 1937 Africans not required as labour on white-owned lands were removed to the reserves, which became increasingly congested.

These land acts were part of a battery of legislation aimed at fostering settler agriculture. Throughout the region white capitalist agriculture was possible only with extensive state support, which was not granted to Africans. African farmers attracted state support only when cattle disease threatened to spread from black areas to white or when soil conservation became a matter of concern. The worldwide depression of the 1930s, which severely affected white farmers, intensified discrimination against African peasant production, and by the 1940s many rural areas were almost entirely dependent on migrant remittances.

Initially, similar policies were pursued north of the Zambezi. In Northern Rhodesia the colonial office attempted to increase settler numbers by opening nearly 12 million acres of the colony's best lands for white farming, while reserves were drawn up for African occupation. Although the reserves were large, like the reserves to the south, they were far from the railway line, contained poor soils, and were soon overcrowded and eroded. It was only after World War II that white landownership was limited in Northern Rhodesia and attempts were made to address African rural poverty.

In the Shire Highlands a handful of settlers owned nearly 34 million acres, while about one-eighth of all land belonged to the African Lakes Company until 1930, when it reverted to customary use. The plantations remained poor and inefficient until the 1920s and '30s, when tobacco and tea replaced coffee and cotton. Low pay, forced-labour practices, and squalid working conditions meant the plantations depended on labour tenants, sharecroppers, and migrants from Mozambique and the more marginal north.

South of the Shire Highlands, however, the administration began to encourage Africans to produce cash crops from about 1910. Despite this evidence of African enterprise, however, racial bias and Nyasaland's poverty tended to handicap peasant agriculture. By the 1930s increased numbers of migrants sought work in South Africa and Rhodesia, especially after the 1913 ban on recruiting "tropical" Africans for the South African mines was lifted.

Despite the status of South West Africa, Africans did not regain the land lost to the Germans; by 1946 the whites (who formed less than one-tenth of the population) controlled over three-fifths of the land

in the Police Zone. Located on arid lands capable
of supporting only sparse human and animal populations, the African reserves served as labour reservoirs, subject to police raids and pass laws. As settler
farms on the better lands in the centre and south of
the territory blocked older patterns of transhumance,
independent pastoral production became difficult.
While a few African families were able to retain their
hold on rural resources, the majority were forced to
seek work in town. Farther north, where the Ovambo
retained control over their more fertile lands, restrictions on their access to markets meant that by the
1930s they, too, were increasingly seeking work in
the colonial economy.

THE INVENTION OF TRIBALISM

In the areas reserved for sole African occupation,
governments made use of African political structures,
creating "tribes" where none had existed and governing through compliant indigenous chiefs and headmen.
Imperial authorities at first sought to curb and undermine the powers of chiefs, whom they saw as the
embodiment of their people and as potential leaders of
resistance; this was as true in the 19th-century Cape
as it was in the Rhodesias and South West Africa in
the early 20th century. Once the powers of the chiefs

had been limited, however, fears of "detribalization" and the potential radicalization of African workers confronted administrations. In response, colonial governments throughout the region moved to bolster chiefs, granting them increased authority over their subjects while seeking to maintain their subordination to the colonial state and establishing local advisory councils as a substitute for popular enfranchisement and representation in central government. This creation of "tribal" institutions frequently created new identities and political interests.

Industrial development and increasing Westernization often made indirect rule through chiefs inappropriate to changing African needs, however. The extension of the market economy intensified divisions, especially as chiefs became identified with unpopular colonial policies and no longer had sufficient land to dispense to their followers. The state recognition of chiefs, the imposition of "tribal boundaries," and land shortages meant that dissatisfied commoners could no longer check arbitrary rule by attaching themselves to alternative polities, as they had in precolonial times. Although urban migration provided some outlet, restrictions on African movement into the colonial towns, together with the often squalid living conditions and low wages, meant that moving to the towns was not an easy option.

LABOUR AND THE MINING INDUSTRY

At the beginning of the 20th century by far the strongest demand for labour came from the gold mines of South Africa. With the creation of the Union of South Africa there was for the first time a state strong enough to ensure the effective implementation of the laws and labour policies that had developed in Kimberley and on the Witwatersrand to control the workforce. The development of South Africa as the most powerful and industrialized country in modern Africa was built upon the labour of a poorly paid, mistreated, and disenfranchised workforce drawn from the entire subcontinent.

The early years of the century also saw intensified recruiting of African labour from Northern Rhodesia, Mozambique, and Nyasaland for the hundreds of small mines working scattered gold deposits in Southern Rhodesia. Because mining profits were so low in Southern Rhodesia, wages, food, housing, and health conditions were cut back ruthlessly, and disease and mortality rates were exceptionally high. Where possible, black workers bypassed the Rhodesian mines and made their way to the Witwatersrand.

Across the Zambezi the absence of mineral wealth meant that Africans in Nyasaland and

Northern Rhodesia migrated to the mines in Katanga (Shaba), Southern Rhodesia, and South Africa in search of money for food and taxation; the opening up of the copper mines shifted some migrant routes to the Copperbelt. In the interwar years Northern Rhodesia and northern Nyasaland were no more than massive labour reservoirs.

In Angola and Mozambique, too, the economy was sustained by labour migration as the recruitment of labour for South African, Rhodesian, and German enterprises provided revenue for tax and trade. The Portuguese government attempted to control the flow of labour from Mozambique to the gold mines through a series of conventions with the South African government. Tax fees on migrants were a major source of state income, while deferred pay ensured the migrant's return, tax payment, and purchase of Portuguese manufactures. Mozambique also received a fixed proportion of the Transvaal's railway traffic. In a similar system in Angola, contract labour was sent to São Tomé; when this system was terminated after allegations of slavery arose in 1908, the São Tomé planters also turned to Mozambique for labour.

Most Mozambican migrant labour came from the region south of the Save River. Farther north the Portuguese had granted wide mining, agricultural, and commercial concessions to chartered companies in the 1890s. Based on the old prazos system, the chartered companies controlled more than half of the colony's lands. Under Salazar the concessions were allowed to expire, but this brought little respite. Southern Mozambique was entrenched as a labour reserve for the Rand; elsewhere in the colony, as in Angola, Africans had to produce fixed quotas of cotton and rice. Confiscations and assaults were legion, despite a plethora of protective legislation. By 1945 more than four-fifths of Portugal's raw cotton came from Mozambique and Angola.

THE IMPACT OF MIGRANT LABOUR

It is difficult to determine the precise impact of migrant labour in Southern Africa in the 20th century. In south-central Africa, for example, the major agricultural communities probably did not send migrants, and the majority of migrants usually came from areas already decimated by slaving and raiding. In other regions, earnings from migrant labour were often used, at least initially, to increase agricultural production, and many migrants maintained their links with the rural areas and retired there in old age. However, many Africans became dependent on the money economy and became locked into the migrant labour system; rural impoverishment resulted from the increasing congestion and soil erosion on the reserves. The division of labour in the countryside began to change, and the burden of agriculture fell increasingly on women and children, although this trend, too, was uneven and may not have existed in some areas until well into the 20th century.

The cheapening of black labour through migrancy rendered skilled white workers vulnerable to attempts by mine owners to reduce costs by substituting cheaper semiskilled black labour for expensive overseas workers. Whites demanded a "colour bar" to protect their access to certain jobs. Initially formulated to reconcile white workers to Milner's decision to import Chinese labour, the colour bar was formally established in South Africa under the Mines and Works Act of 1911 and its amendment in 1926. At the same time, industrial conciliation legislation introduced after a 1922 strike excluded blacks from the wage-bargaining machinery. These examples were followed in the Rhodesias as well, although in the Copperbelt white workers were weaker and the liberal impulse of government stronger, so that by the 1950s a skilled black workforce began to emerge there.

URBANIZATION AND MANUFACTURING

Mining shaped Southern Africa's experience of industrialization, although during the 19th century towns in the Cape and Natal engaged in small-scale manufacturing. This accelerated in response to the demands of the mining industry, but not until World War I did manufacturing make a significant contribution to the economy. By the end of the war the future of the mining industry seemed to be in doubt, while dispossessed rural Afrikaners began to enter the cities in search of work. The state thus encouraged the development of the manufacturing industry.

Although the plight of poor Afrikaners was frequently attributed to their refusal to do manual labour, they were at a double disadvantage in the towns. Unlike Africans—who had some access to the land—Afrikaners were totally dependent on their urban wages and lacked the skills of English-speaking workers. It was in response to this that the "civilized labour" policy, which favoured employers using white labour, was devised in the 1920s. The policy probably was more effective in spurring capital-intensive manufacturing and the employment of poorly paid Afrikaner women than in eliminating white poverty: by 1930 one in five Afrikaners was classified as "poor white." They formed an important constituency for the anti-imperialism of Afrikaner nationalism, which developed in the interwar years.

To meet the needs of Afrikaners in the cities, South Africa from 1924 promoted manufacturing through a number of techniques: the levying of tariffs, the use of the gold tax to subsidize infra-structure development, the provision of inexpensive food to manufacturing workers, and the imposition of stringent controls to ensure low wages for black labourers. However, the insulation of South Africa's fledgling industries from international competition during the worldwide depression and World War II may have been the most important factor in its economic expansion. Although Southern Rhodesia attempted some of the same strategies, its economy remained overshadowed by South Africa even after the establishment of the British Central African Federation in 1953. The development of manufac-turing in South Africa and Southern Rhodesia led to a sharp increase in the number of urban Africans in both territories. Until the war years their welfare needs were largely ignored.

THE AFRICAN RESPONSE

African peoples, who were so painfully drawn into the capitalist economy of Southern Africa and were subjected to ever-increasing administrative, economic, and political control, did not acquiesce in their subordination without resistance. Most engaged in daily struggles to survive and devised individual strategies to resist exploitation. Yet they did not all experience their subjection in the same way, and to some extent this weakened resistance. The 20th century witnessed the rise of new classes, with the emergence of an African petite bourgeoisie and working class in the towns and a considerable degree of stratification in the countryside. Migrant labour both undermined and strengthened the authority of the chiefs, especially in areas where the colonial state was anxious to retain traditional structures for purposes of social control. Alongside the growth of nationalist movements among the educated elite and the organization of trade unions among workers, there was a continuation of royal family politics, a restructuring of ethnic identification, and a resort to millenarian solutions.

ROYAL FAMILY POLITICS

In regions where large centralized states had existed at the time of the colonial takeover, royal politics continued to be of significance. In Barotseland, Swaziland, and Basutoland, where paramount chiefs were recognized by the British, the traditional aristocracy combined with the educated elite to protect their position and demand the redress of grievances. In both Matabeleland and Zululand, where the royal families had been militarily defeated, royalists combined to demand state recognition of the monarchy, while in Nyasaland in the 1930s there was an attempt to create a Tonga paramountcy and to restore the Ngoni king. The struggle for the recognition of the monarchy had anticolonial overtones. In general, the monarchies were most successful in the climate of indirect rule of the 1930s and in areas where settlers were weak.

POLITICAL ORGANIZATIONS AND TRADE UNIONS

Nonviolent African opposition to white rule— through the adoption of Western-style political organizations and the formation of trade unions— was longest and most intense south of the Limpopo, where the existence of substantial Coloured and Indian minorities gave an extra dimension to anticolonialism. In South Africa, between 1906 and 1913, Mahatma Gandhi formed the South African

Indian Congress and led the first large-scale nonviolent resistance campaign against anti-Indian legislation. Gandhi gained limited success, although restrictions on Indian movement and immigration to South Africa remained in force. After his departure in 1914, however, the militancy of the Indian Congress was lost until after World War II, when younger, more radical groups won power from the middle class that had dominated the organization. Nevertheless, Gandhi's example influenced later African nationalists.

The Coloureds of the Cape and Transvaal also mobilized politically in the first nationwide black political organization, the African Political Organization (APO; later African People's Organization), founded in 1902, which sought to unite Africans in opposition to the South Africa Act of 1909. The formation of a separate Coloured Affairs Department to some extent diverted Coloured political energies from joint black action. Coloureds were prominent, however, in the All-African Convention, a body formed in 1935 that represented numerous African organizations. In 1943 the All-African Convention, along with several Coloured organizations, founded the Non-European Unity Movement, which rejected cooperation with the government and sought full democratic rights for all South Africans.

In 1912 educated Africans united various welfare associations, which had developed in the late 19th and early 20th centuries, into the South African Native National Congress (later the African National Congress [ANC]). They aimed to represent African grievances, overcome tribal divisions, and gain acceptance from whites through self-help, education, and the accumulation of property. Demands for industrial education, individual land tenure, and representation in Parliament were accompanied by attacks on the pass laws, the colour bar, and the Native Lands Act of 1913; until the 1940s the ANC's methods remained strictly constitutional and appealed mainly to the educated elite.

The ANC had its counterparts farther to the north, partly because many early nationalists had either studied or worked in South Africa. Native associations and welfare associations evolved among the educated elite from the second decade of the 20th century and gave birth to congresses in Southern Rhodesia in 1934, Nyasaland in 1944, and Northern Rhodesia in 1948, all forerunners of more radical anticolonial movements. Despite regional differences, the class composition and methods of struggle of these organizations were broadly similar until the 1950s, with the South African organizations leading the way.

Although Africans in South Africa were moving into industry by the end of World War I, their trade unions were hampered by pass laws, lack of recognition, and police harassment; strikes were illegal and often were put down with violence. Nevertheless, the period 1918–22 saw a great deal of working-class militancy, and in 1920 Clements Kadalie, a Nyasaland migrant, founded the Industrial and Commercial Workers' Union (ICU). Initially consisting of dockworkers in Cape Town, the ICU spread rapidly as a mass movement in the towns and countryside, where those who had been evicted responded with millenarian zeal to its message. At its height the ICU claimed 100,000 members and had branches as far afield as Southern Rhodesia and South West Africa, but it had largely disintegrated by 1929. By then the Communist Party of South Africa was organizing black workers. Black unions appeared elsewhere in the region after World War II.

From the early 1920s the South African government, seeking to preempt black radicalism, attempted to provide channels for the expression of African grievances through a variety of local consultative councils. In the Rhodesias and Nyasaland and, slightly later, in the smaller colonial territories, advisory councils, "tribal representatives," and rural "native authorities" played a similar role.

In Angola and Mozambique Africans had even fewer political rights, except for a brief republican period (1910–26) when political organizations, trade unions, and the press flourished. For a while it appeared that Africans and settlers in Angola would strive for similar reformist goals, but the Africans broke away to form organizations publicizing black grievances and demanding limited welfare and educational benefits. Crushed even before the advent of Salazar, these groups were revived as social and educational organizations, and it was only during the 1950s that they became overtly political.

THE IMPACT OF WORLD WAR II

Unlike World War I, World War II did not involve campaigns on Southern African soil, although large numbers of black and white soldiers fought elsewhere in Africa. Yet in many ways this war had a greater impact. In South Africa manufacturing overtook mining and agriculture in its contribution to the economy, and large numbers of Africans settled permanently in the major cities. In Southern Rhodesia, too, the war boosted the economy, and by its end tobacco farming and secondary industry had emerged as key economic sectors.

Economic expansion during the war led to increased organization among African workers, whose wages lagged far behind the rising cost of living. In South Africa these years saw a wave of African worker militancy, partly inspired by the Communist Party, and a reorganization of the African National Congress by a new, younger urban constituency. The brutal suppression of a 1946 strike by African mine workers further radicalized many African nationalists and brought about a closer alliance between the ANC and the Communist Party. This alliance became even more important after the banning of the party in 1950.

In south-central Africa, too, the end of the war brought an eruption of strikes, particularly a strike by railway workers in 1945, which led to the founding of a large number of African trade unions in Southern Rhodesia. In 1947 the British government dispatched a trade unionist to organize African mine workers in the Copperbelt, while the first union in Nyasaland followed in 1949. With general strikes in Bulawayo and Salisbury in 1948, a new form of political action had emerged.

World War II was important in shaking up the politics of the region in other ways as well. Thousands of Africans had joined the army, and some came back home with widened horizons, while their experiences of demobilization and discriminatory compensation fueled nationalist feeling. The 1941 Atlantic Charter, which proclaimed the right of all peoples to self-determination, also stimulated political activists in Southern Africa. In the 1940s the African National Congress began to demand full democratic rights in South Africa for the first time, and its influence, like that of the trade unions, began to be felt throughout the region, spread partly by returning migrant labourers, who formed similar organizations in neighbouring territories.

For those territories under the authority of the British colonial office, the Colonial Development and Welfare Acts of 1940 and 1945 signaled Britain's commitment to the development of empire at a time of internal weakness. Thus, after the war Britain attempted to expand agricultural production through agricultural research stations, extension programs, promotion of technology, and conservation measures. These efforts largely benefited white estate owners rather than African peasants, however, and the attempted restructuring of peasant production prompted considerable rural unrest, providing anticolonial movements throughout the region with a large, disaffected constituency.

INDEPENDENCE AND DECOLONIZATION IN SOUTHERN AFRICA

After the war the imperial powers were under strong international pressure to decolonize. In Southern Africa, however, the transfer of power to an African majority was greatly complicated by the presence of entrenched white settlers. After an initial phase from 1945 to about 1958, in which white power seemed to be consolidated, decolonization proceeded in three stages: first, the relatively peaceful achievement by 1968 of independence by those territories under direct British rule (the High Commission territories became Lesotho, Botswana, and Swaziland, and Northern Rhodesia and Nyasaland became Zambia and Malawi); second, the far bloodier struggle for independence in the Portuguese colonies and in Southern Rhodesia (from 1965 Rhodesia, which achieved independence as Zimbabwe in 1980); and, third, the denouement in South West Africa (which in 1990 achieved independence as Namibia) and in South Africa, where the black majority took power after nonracial, democratic elections in 1994. While at the end of the colonial period imperial interests still controlled the economies of the region, by the end of the 20th century South Africa had become the dominant economic power. The beginning of the 21st century ushered in attempts to finally create unity among all the countries in Southern Africa. Despite the spread of multiparty democracy, however, violence, inequality, and poverty persisted throughout the region.

THE CONSOLIDATION OF WHITE RULE IN SOUTHERN AFRICA

Paradoxically, World War II and the rise of more radical African political movements initially consolidated white rule in Southern Africa, as evidenced by the victory of the predominantly Afrikaner National Party in South Africa, the creation of the Central African Federation by Britain, and renewed white immigration to the Rhodesias, Angola, Mozambique, and South West Africa. Once again, developments in South Africa dominated the region, although the discrediting of racism in Europe and decolonization in South Asia led to increasing international censure of South African racial policies.

Dissatisfaction with the wartime cabinet and fears of urban African militants lay behind the victory of the Reunited National Party (later the National Party [NP]), which ran on a platform of apartheid ("apartness") in the white elections of 1948. Although the

NP won only a plurality of votes, its victory signified a new Afrikaner unity that resulted from 30 years of intense ideological labour and institution building by ethnic nationalists intent on capturing the South African state.

Although the various interests in the NP had different interpretations of apartheid, the party essentially had three connected goals: to entrench

The apartheid policy governed relations between South Africa's white minority and nonwhite majority. It sanctioned racial segregation and political and economic discrimination against nonwhites.

itself in power, to promote Afrikaner concerns, and to protect white supremacy. By 1970 these goals largely had been achieved. The NP controlled parliament, and many English speakers voted for the Nationalists—despite their declaration of a republic in 1960–61 and subsequent decision to remove South Africa from the British Commonwealth—believing that the NP alone ensured white domination. Economic and educational policies favoured Afrikaners, who became increasingly urbanized and less economically disadvantaged.

Under Hendrik Verwoerd, who served as minister of Native Affairs and later as prime minister (1958–66), apartheid took shape. Controls over African labour mobility were tightened, and the colour bar in employment was extended. From 1959 chiefly authorities in the rural reserves (renamed "Bantu homelands" or Bantustans) were given increased powers and granted limited self-government, though they remained subject to white control. Ethnic and racial distinctions among whites, Africans, Coloureds, and Indians were more strictly defined and policed. Although Coloureds and Indians were subordinated to white rule and humiliated by racial discrimination, they nevertheless were privileged in comparison with Africans.

Black opposition to apartheid policies in the 1950s was led by the ANC in alliance with other opposition organizations consisting of radical whites, Coloureds, and Indians. In 1955 this Congress Alliance drew up the Freedom Charter, a program of nonracial social democracy. Africanist suspicion of nonracialism and hostility to white Communists, however, led to the formation of the rival Pan-Africanist Congress (PAC) in 1959. Both organizations were banned after demonstrations against the pass laws in March 1960 at Sharpeville, in which police killed at least 67 and injured more than 180 African protestors, triggering massive protests. Increasingly draconian security legislation, the banning, exile, and imprisonment of leaders (including Nelson Mandela, the leader of the ANC), and the widespread use of informants resulted in a period of relative political calm in the 1960s.

The stability of the 1960s encouraged international investment, and the South African economy became far more centralized and capital-intensive. Economic growth made possible unprecedented social engineering, and the political geography of South Africa was transformed as millions of people were removed from so-called white areas to the black homelands. Access to welfare and political rights were made dependent on state-manipulated ethnic identities, which assumed new importance with the creation of the homelands. In 1976 the Transkei homeland was given independence by the South African government, and grants of "independence" followed over the next four years to Bophuthatswana, Ciskei, and Venda, though their "independence" was not internationally recognized.

LESOTHO, BOTSWANA, AND SWAZILAND

The victory of the overtly republican National Party in South Africa challenged British interests in the subcontinent. The NP's economic policies appeared to threaten British investments in South Africa at a time when Britain was particularly dependent on its colonial possessions for its sterling balances, while the Nationalists also renewed their demand for the incorporation into South Africa of Lesotho, Botswana, and Swaziland.

By the mid 1950s it was clear that the three High Commission territories could not be transferred to South Africa and had to be prepared for independence. Limited funds were made available for the provision of social services, education, soil conservation, and infrastructure development, but this assistance did little to reduce the territories' dependence on migrant labour to South Africa. A partial exception was Swaziland, where British- and South African–owned asbestos and coal mines, sugar and timber plantations, and cattle ranches had begun to generate more local jobs after the war.

The independence of the majority of Britain's African territories put the independence of the High Commission territories in Southern Africa on the British agenda, despite their continued economic dependence on South Africa and the relative weakness of their independence movements.

Lesotho, with high levels of literacy, was the first to organize. In 1952 Ntsu Mokhehle formed the Basutoland Congress Party (BCP), modeled on the ANC. In 1958 Chief Leabua Jonathan, who was to become Lesotho's first prime minister, founded the conservative Basutoland National Party (BNP), with the support of the South African government, the powerful Roman Catholic church, and the queen regent. Jonathan led the BNP to a narrow victory in the 1965 elections; Lesotho achieved independence in 1966. In Botswana and Swaziland, modern nationalist movements emerged somewhat later and were dominated by members of the royal families, who were able to perpetuate monarchical domination quite effectively through the ballot box. In Botswana, which achieved its independence in 1966, Seretse Khama—the grandson of the Ngwato chief Khama III—emerged as the first president. In Swaziland, where the presence of white settlers and South African and international economic interests held up full independence until 1968, the Swazi king Sobhuza II emerged as head of state through the overwhelming electoral majority of his Imbokodvo National Movement in the rural areas. Thus, in all three territories conservative governments anxious to avoid provoking South Africa emerged in the first elections after independence.

Botswana was undoubtedly the most successful economically and politically and retained the most open political institutions and the most distance from South Africa. Dominated by a modernizing elite, the country's economy flourished with the expansion of cattle ranching and diamond, nickel, and copper mining. Botswana played a leading role in efforts to coordinate the regional economy. The BCP, with a primarily rural electoral base, ruled Botswana into the mid 1990s.

In Swaziland, Sobhuza II in 1973 declared a state of emergency, suspended the constitution, dissolved parliament and all political parties, and consolidated his rule after a more radical opposition party showed strength in the 1972 elections. In 1978 a new constitution ensured the continued power of the monarchy in alliance with selected chiefs. This ruling elite used its domination of the state and land to accumulate wealth in close collaboration with foreign (mainly South African) investors. Until the death of Sobhuza II in 1982, all opposition to the government and to its close links with South Africa was suppressed. In the 1980s and '90s political repression and competition for power within the ruling group intensified.

Fears that the more radical BCP would win the 1970 elections in Lesotho led Jonathan, supported by South Africa, to declare a state of emergency, annul the election, and suspend the constitution. Opposition leaders fled, and by the late 1970s chronic warfare had erupted in Lesotho's northeastern mountains. Through the 1960s and early '70s Jonathan was South Africa's most reliable regional ally, but he subsequently became an outspoken critic of South African policies. Jonathan's authoritarian rule continued until 1986, when he was deposed in a military coup supported by South Africa.

THE CENTRAL AFRICAN FEDERATION

Alarm at the NP victory in South Africa also stimulated Britain into federating its south-central African territories as a bulwark against Afrikaner nationalism. Even before World War II, Northern Rhodesian whites had begun to consider federation with Southern Rhodesia as a response to growing African assertiveness, and support for federation increased after the war. At the same time, the growing importance of the copper industry in Northern Rhodesia attracted Southern Rhodesian whites to the idea of federation. Wartime collaboration promoted federal ideas among white settlers and in British government circles. It was widely assumed that Southern Rhodesia would provide managerial and administrative skills, Northern Rhodesia copper revenues, and Nyasaland labour for the new entity. Africans in the north, however, feared that federation would prevent political advance and extend Southern Rhodesia's racist laws. Ignoring African opposition, in 1953 Britain's Conservative government brought the territories together in the Federation of Rhodesia and Nyasaland, commonly known as the Central African Federation.

Prosperity muted African protest in the early years of federation, although dissent mounted in the impoverished reserves of Southern Rhodesia, where disaffection was fueled by attempts to restructure peasant production at a time of growing landlessness and congestion on inferior land. Despite the rhetoric of multiracial partnership, the economic advantages of federation appeared mainly to benefit Southern Rhodesian whites.

MALAWI AND ZAMBIA

By the late 1950s more militant national movements had emerged in the Central African Federation and were attempting to mobilize a disaffected peasantry in all three territories. The emergence of these nationalist movements profoundly disturbed the federal authorities. After sporadic unrest in Nyasaland in 1959 a state of emergency was declared, while in all three territories nationalist leaders were arrested and their organizations banned. The crackdown set off further disorder, and in the northern territories the British were persuaded to move toward decolonization. By 1961–62 the nationalists had been released and new constitutions drawn

Kenneth Kaunda's inspired opposition to British colonial policies made him the leader of Zambia's independence movement. He was elected as the country's first president in 1964.

up, and in 1963 the federation was dissolved. In the following year the Malawi Congress Party under Hastings Kamuzu Banda and the United National Independence Party (UNIP) under Kenneth Kaunda won the first universal suffrage elections in Nyasaland and Northern Rhodesia, respectively, and led them into independence as Malawi and Zambia.

Banda and Kaunda differed greatly in their relations with the liberation struggles in the rest of Southern Africa. In the hope of gaining control of northern Mozambique, Banda negotiated with the Portuguese and withheld assistance from Mozambican nationalists, who during the 1960s were beginning their military campaign. He also established close ties with the white South African government, which supplied much of Malawi's direct aid. Malawi thus became the foundation of South Africa's "outward-looking" foreign policy in Africa.

Although initially Zambia was as tied economically to Rhodesia and the Portuguese colonies, Kaunda backed the resistance movements there and supported United Nations (UN) sanctions against the white government in Rhodesia. He paid a heavy price. The sanctions closed Zambia's major trade and transportation routes through Rhodesia, and, although alternate routes were established through Angola and new east-west lines through Tanzania

MADAGASCAR

Despite its location, Madagascar is not always considered part of Southern Africa because of its distinct language and cultural heritage. The first European known to have visited the island was Portuguese navigator Diogo Dias, in 1500. It was called the Isle of St. Lawrence by the Portuguese, who frequently raided Madagascar during the 16th century, attempting to destroy the incipient Muslim settlements there. The French, driven by an interest in trade, established settlements on the island starting in the 17th century.

The French took complete control by 1898, abolishing the Merina monarchy (that native kingdom had conquered large parts of the island) after several decades of fighting for control of the island. The teaching of French in the schools was made compulsory. Customs duties favoured French products, though Malagasy enterprise was also encouraged. Exports were confined to agricultural products and raw materials for industry. Three-quarters of all trade was with France. Aspects of life became Westernized, especially in the cities, and half the population became Christian.

In 1915 a nationalist secret society, the Vy Vato Sakelika (VVS), was outlawed. In 1920 a teacher, Jean Ralaimongo, launched a campaign in the press to give the Malagasy "subjects" French citizenship and to make Madagascar a French département. When France failed to respond, the movement turned toward nationalism. The constitution of 1946, creating the French Union, made Madagascar an overseas territory of the French Republic, with representatives to the Paris assemblies and a local assembly at Antananarivo. The political struggle erupted into violence on March 30, 1947, with a full-scale insurrection in eastern Madagascar. The leaders of the Democratic Movement for Malagasy Renewal (Mouvement Démocratique de la Rénovation Malgache) were outlawed. While an official count of lives lost in the revolt records about 11,000 dead, it is certain that thousands more of the Malagasy populace perished from famine, cold, and psychological misery while hiding from both the French army and the insurgents in the island's inhospitable tropical forests.

A period of political inactivity followed until the 1950s. After the Overseas Territories Law of 1956 gave Madagascar an executive elected by the local assembly, Vice-Premier Philibert Tsiranana founded the Social Democratic Party (Parti Social

(CONTINUED ON THE NEXT PAGE)

(CONTINUED FROM THE PREVIOUS PAGE)

Démocrate; PSD), which, though most of its members were non-Merina from the coastal areas, offered to cooperate with the Merina. In 1958 France agreed to let its overseas territories decide their own fate. In a referendum on September 28, Madagascar voted for autonomy within the French Community. On October 14, 1958, the autonomous Malagasy Republic was proclaimed; Tsiranana headed the provisional government.

The opposition regrouped under the name Congress Party for the Independence of Madagascar (Antokon'ny Kongresin'ny Fahaleovantenan'i Madagasikara; AKFM), which included both Protestant Merina dissidents and communists. Antananarivo was the party's stronghold; it also had some support in the provinces but, owing to the electoral system established by the PSD, held only three seats in the legislature.

The PSD also settled the provincial question: executive power in the local assemblies was vested in a minister delegated by the central government. Tsiranana was elected president of the republic, and he was instrumental in obtaining its independence on June 26, 1960. Tsiranana and the PSD remained in power until 1972. Under his regime, successive development plans were inspired, according to Tsiranana, by a "grassroots socialism" and were aimed at improving the lot of the peasantry.

were constructed by the mid 1970s, subsequent armed incursions from Rhodesia and South Africa and continued warfare in Angola and Mozambique disrupted the costly new trade and transportation lines. Zambia's economy contracted by nearly half between 1974 and 1979, and its collapse was prevented only by intervention from the International Monetary Fund (IMF).

During the late 1970s Malawi, long believed to have successful rural development policies, also faced economic crisis. The lean years of the 1980s saw a widening gap between rich and poor, which was made worse by Banda's support of the Mozambican insurgency movement Renamo and the influx of vast numbers of refugees from the civil war in Mozambique.

ANGOLA AND MOZAMBIQUE

White power in Angola and Mozambique remained relatively weak in comparison with South Africa and South West Africa. After the war Portugal sought to maintain its colonies in the face of growing, if still slight, African urban nationalist movements by increasing the settler population dramatically. This was facilitated in Angola by a coffee boom and the discovery of minerals and petroleum and in Mozambique by government-instituted agricultural schemes.

These developments brought little benefit to the majority of Africans, however, who continued to work as ill-paid migrant labourers, their upward mobility blocked by settlers. Even in areas of limited fertility, Africans still had to produce their quota of cotton, rice, or coffee; most of the good land was taken over by wealthy white landowners and multinational companies, and the forced labour codes remained in operation until 1962.

The longest, most divided, and bloodiest wars against colonialism in the subcontinent occurred in the Portuguese colonies. War first erupted in Angola in 1961, in a series of apparently unconnected uprisings. The initiative was captured by the urban-based Popular Liberation Movement of Angola (Movimento Popular de Libertação de Angola; MPLA), under its poet-president Agostinho Neto. The MPLA was supported by communists in Portugal, the Soviet Union, and Cuba, but its hegemony was contested from the start by Holden Roberto's National Front for the Liberation of Angola (Frente Nacional de Libertação de Angola; FNLA), based in Congo (Kinshasa), and by Jonas Savimbi's National Union for the Total Independence of Angola (União Nacional para a Independência Total de Angola; UNITA), supported primarily by Ovimbundu in the south.

Agostinho Neto first became known in 1948, when he published a volume of poems in Luanda and joined a national cultural movement that was aimed at rediscovering indigenous Angolan culture.

In Mozambique the nationalist organizations were initially more successfully united. The anti-colonial struggle was led by Eduardo Mondlane of the Mozambique Liberation Front (Frente da Liber-tação de Moçambique; Frelimo), which was formed in 1962 by exiles in Tanzania. Internal dissent had been crushed by 1964, and Frelimo launched a guerrilla war against targets in northern Mozam-bique, claiming to have established its own admin-istrative, educational, and economic networks in the northern districts. Despite the assassination of Mondlane in 1969, a new phase of the war opened in 1971 under the leadership of Samora Machel, and by 1974 Frelimo controlled much of northern and central Mozambique.

Portugal's initial response to the outbreak of revolt in Angola and Mozambique was all-out war, and by the mid 1960s there were some 70,000 Por-tuguese troops in each territory. Large numbers of black troops were recruited, and villagers supporting the guerrillas were subjected to savage reprisals. In a bid to attract international support, Portugal opened the colonies to foreign investment in 1963, and by the late 1960s the regime also instituted modest eco-nomic and educational reforms to preempt the na-tionalists and meet rising demands for a semiskilled workforce. But the reforms were too few and too late, and in April 1974 the sheer cost of the wars—together with rising dissatisfaction with the government in Portugal—led to an army coup, the collapse of the Portuguese government, and Portuguese withdrawal from Africa.

When the Portuguese left Luanda in November 1975, Angola was in the throes of a civil war between its divided liberation movements. The war escalated as the United States aided the FNLA-UNITA alliance through Zaire and encouraged a South African invasion of Angola in 1974–75 in the hope of installing a pro-Western government. The Soviet Union supplied weapons to the MPLA, which was aided by Cuban troops. The South African invasion was repelled, but South Africa continued to destabilize the MPLA government over the next 15 years through its covert support for UNITA, which it hoped to install as its client. The MPLA eventually established control of Angola under Neto, but its government was undermined by South African incursions, the flight of most of the settlers at independence, incursions of Kongo peoples from Congo (Kinshasa), hostility from the United States, and its own doctrinaire economic policies.

Portuguese withdrawal also led to Mozambique's independence under a Frelimo government in June 1975, but the flight of skilled expatriates and Mozambique's proximity to hostile regimes in South Africa and Rhodesia caused immediate problems. The country was severely hit by a drastic cutback in recruitment by the South African Chamber of Mines in 1976 and, like Zambia, paid heavily for obeying UN sanctions against Rhodesia and for supporting the liberation movements. Nevertheless, in the early years of independence, Frelimo abolished many of the most hated aspects of colonial rule and greatly increased the availability of welfare resources for the black populace. Mozambican territory was raided by Rhodesia and South Africa in 1979, and this was followed by further South African attacks and the infiltration of the Mozambican National Resistance (Resistência Nacional Moçambicana; Renamo), a brutal insurgency group established by Rhodesian intelligence services in 1976–77.

In Mozambique and Angola the unpopularity of the governments' Marxist policies—including the concentration of the population in communal villages, state farms, and cooperatives and attacks on private property, chiefly authority, and religion—eased the way for South African intervention. During the 1980s both Frelimo and the MPLA lost control outside the main urban areas.

ZIMBABWE

African liberation in Rhodesia was closely tied to the independence struggles in Mozambique. The election of 1962—boycotted by African nationalists—was won by the extreme right-wing Rhodesian Front (RF) party, which ran on a platform of immediate independence under white control. The Central African Federation was dissolved in 1963. Britain was unwilling to grant Rhodesia independence; in 1965 the RF, under the leadership of Ian Smith, unilaterally declared Rhodesia independent. Under the RF, government policies came even closer to those in South Africa. Although Rhodesia had an ostensibly colour-blind franchise, less than 1 percent of Africans were able to vote. The powers of chiefs were bolstered and discriminatory legislation increased. Despite international pressure, Britain refused to use force against the illegal regime. International economic sanctions were undermined by South Africa, Portugal, and multinational oil companies. White commercial agriculture was heavily subsidized and competed with African peasants, who felt the main burden of the sanctions.

The banning of successive nationalist organizations and the detention and exile of their leadership led to fierce infighting and the emergence of two major liberation organizations, the Zimbabwe African National Union (ZANU), under Robert Mugabe, and the Zimbabwe African People's Union (ZAPU), under Joshua Nkomo. With Frelimo's military successes in northeastern Mozambique in 1971–72 and, more important, with the transformation of the power structure in the region after the independence of the Portuguese territories, a new guerrilla strategy began to make headway. Various attempts by the British to resolve the conflict—including a referendum on a new constitution in 1972—all failed, and by the late 1970s the Rhodesian army and the guerrillas pursued the war with increasing ferocity, both sides often intimidating and torturing recruits in the rural areas.

By 1978 it had become clear that the Rhodesian government would not win the war, and Smith, under pressure from Western countries and South Africa, agreed in 1978 to allow the internal African opposition to contest multiracial elections the following year. These elections, however, excluded ZAPU and ZANU. Thus, despite the appointment of a black prime minister, the war continued unabated. In 1979 renewed negotiations in London ultimately led to a peace settlement that established majority rule, and in 1980 Mugabe and ZANU won a landslide electoral victory.

The release of a large number of unemployed, armed young men into the countryside bequeathed a violent legacy, and by 1982 the initial ZANU-ZAPU government coalition broke down in the face of increasing violence in Matabeleland, for which ZANU held ZAPU responsible. Early in 1983 Mugabe sent government forces to punish the people of Matabeleland. Despite the withdrawal of troops and an amnesty in 1988, memories of this brutal counterinsurgency campaign were even more traumatic than recollections of the liberation struggle.

The idea of a one-party state was dropped amid calls for reparations for the massacres in Matabeleland and for greater public accountability. While the early years of Zimbabwean independence were economically promising, with the return of investment as sanctions were lifted and a series of good harvests, much of the white economy and bureaucracy remained intact, and gross inequalities persisted. Despite its revolutionary rhetoric, ZANU (which ruled Zimbabwe into the mid 1990s) was more intent on replacing white government with black than on transforming the lives of the poor.

NAMIBIA

In South West Africa, too, the National Party increased its control in the 1950s and '60s. Long governed as part of South Africa, in 1949 South West Africa became South Africa's fifth province, and its white population was swollen by about 3,000 immigrants. The economy grew dramatically, increasing the mobility of black workers and creating an urban-based black intelligentsia for the first time. Apartheid was extended to South West Africa, however, and in the mid 1960s its reserves were also consolidated into seven ethnically defined homelands under tribal authorities.

The small political associations in South West Africa after the war were profoundly influenced by their South African counterparts, but the first mass organization to protest against South Africa's policies was formed only in 1958; in 1960 this organization became the South West Africa People's Organization (SWAPO). Launched by Ovambo contract workers, SWAPO came to represent most black South West Africans in opposing apartheid, racial inequalities, and economic subordination to South Africa. After years of fruitless peaceful protest, SWAPO began a military campaign against the government in 1966.

Although South Africa did not recognize the authority of the UN, the issue of South African rule in South West Africa came before the UN regularly, and in 1966 the UN called for complete South African withdrawal. This decision was upheld by the International Court of Justice at The Hague in 1971. In 1973 the UN appointed its own commissioner for Namibia (as the territory became known in the 1970s); despite the presence of the UN commissioner and the intensification of SWAPO's military campaign, it was only after Angolan independence in 1975 and increasing international pressure that South Africa's policies began to change.

The independence of Angola prompted changes in South African strategy toward Namibia during the late 1970s, as South Africa attempted to transform the territory into a quasi-independent buffer against more radical change by proposing complex constitutional arrangements for a transitional government. The strategy, based on the co-option of a local black elite as a moderate alternative to SWAPO, was intended to placate international opinion while leaving control of Namibia in South African hands and keeping its military options open. The constitutional proposals were rejected by the international community, however, and in 1978 the UN Security Council passed Resolution 435, which set out proposals for a cease-fire and UN-supervised elections. South Africa did not move to implement this resolution, though it had accepted similar proposals earlier.

By the second half of the 1980s—in part because South Africa once more had been drawn into invading Angola—the war in Namibia was becoming increasingly costly for South Africa in military, political, economic, and diplomatic terms. A turning point occurred in 1988 when the South African Defense Force's inability to take Cuito-Cuanavale in Angola revealed South Africa's lack of superior airpower and its inadequate weapons technology. Under joint pressure from the Soviet Union and the United States, South Africa finally agreed to implement Resolution 435, and democratic elections in 1989 were won by SWAPO, led by Sam Nujoma. In 1990 Namibia finally achieved independence.

SOUTH AFRICA

The process of decolonization in south-central Africa and the High Commission territories was generally peaceful. By the late 1960s the few remaining nonindependent African countries were all located in settler-dominated Southern Africa. The 1970s were a time of escalating wars of liberation in Mozambique, Angola, Namibia, and Zimbabwe. The independence of the Portuguese colonies under self-styled Marxist governments was crucial in shifting the balance of power against the remaining white minority states in the subcontinent. International involvement in the region increased, and by 1980 only South Africa and Namibia remained under minority rule.

For the territories of Southern Africa, the continuance of apartheid in South Africa shaped the postindependence years; the liberation of these territories in turn inspired and politicized South Africa's black populace and transformed the balance of power in the region. In response, P.W. Botha, who became prime minister of South Africa in 1978 and led South Africa until 1989, massively increased defense expenditures and began a low-grade war on the neighbouring states, determined to destroy all ANC bases. At the same time, Botha pursued an internal program of con-stitutional reform, which strengthened the powers of the state president and increased repression of the black majority. The South African military assumed greater political importance. South Af-rica destabilized the region by arming internal dissidents, who attacked schools, clinics, railways, and harbours. This intervention was especially devastating in Angola and Mozambique, but South Africa also destabilized eastern Zimbabwe and raided alleged ANC bases in Zambia, Botswana, Swaziland, and Lesotho.

For all the apparent success of its social engineering policies, by the late 1960s cracks had begun to appear in the National Party's edifice of control. It subsequently confronted multiple crises, as black opposition again broke to the surface with the emergence of the Black Consciousness movement in 1968, led by the charismatic activist Stephen Biko. The movement sought to raise black self-awareness and to unite black students, professionals, and intellectuals. As black political activity increased, the apparently monolithic NP began to fragment.

The economy also began to show signs of weakness by the mid 1970s. Inflation climbed steeply and the economy contracted; a reliance on imported technology contributed to a trade deficit. Whites, who constituted a declining proportion of the population, could not meet the demand for skilled and semiskilled labour. The small internal market and African trade sanctions also hampered growth.

Yet the economic growth of the 1960s had expanded the black working class and increased its confidence, and 1972–73 saw a wave of strikes and rapid growth of the trade union movement. In some sectors the labour activism caused African wages to rise more quickly than white wages. Nevertheless, technological innovation led to high unemployment for the unskilled, and urban conditions for Africans continued to deteriorate as impoverished homeland inhabitants defied the pass laws and sought work in town. For them, the fiction of the independence of the homelands came to have a grim reality in the 1980s, as their homeland citizenship restricted their legal access to jobs and housing in the rest of South Africa.

The revival of labour activism and the independence of Mozambique and Angola further inspired the Black Consciousness movement. In June 1976 the government's determination to impose Afrikaans on black schools provided the flashpoint for prolonged countrywide protests, touched off after police fired on demonstrating students in Soweto (a black township outside Johannesburg). This event transformed political consciousness beyond the youth—although they remained in the forefront of protest thereafter—with far-reaching consequences. Churches were radicalized, large numbers of community organizations sprang up, and there was a resurgence of support for the banned ANC, particularly among young people. By the late 1970s the ANC had decided to reorganize its underground internally, emphasizing political organization within the country.

In response, the government abandoned many aspects of orthodox apartheid: African trade unions were recognized, the pass laws were abolished, and attempts were made to co-opt the African middle and skilled working class (through the granting of limited urban and welfare rights) and to enhance the status of Indians and Coloureds (through constitutional change). The result was to politicize civil society even further, as the state was seen as using welfare for purposes of social control. Government attempts

Nelson Mandela was imprisoned by the South African government for more than 25 years. Here he celebrates his release on February 11, 1990, with his wife, Winnie, and other supporters.

to address problems almost invariably led to fresh confrontations with the alienated black population.

The reform process had stalled by the mid 1980s, and the state attempted to undermine black opposition by cultivating conservative African leaders, notably Chief Mangosuthu Buthelezi, head of the primarily Zulu Inkatha movement in Natal, which became the scene of internecine violence. When F.W. de Klerk ascended to the presidency in 1989, he faced continuing African militancy, international economic and cultural sanctions, renewed economic recession, and intensifying war in Angola and Namibia.

On February 2, 1990, de Klerk announced his intention to free Nelson Mandela, lift the ban on many opposition parties (including the ANC and the PAC), and negotiate with the black majority for a new, nonracial constitution. Agreement on an interim constitution was reached in 1993, and in April 1994 Mandela was elected president of South Africa.

CONCLUSION

Historians will long debate the heritage of economic development, mass bitterness, and cultural cleavage that colonialism has left to the world, but the political problems of decolonization in Africa were grave and immediate.

The African continent had been divided into small geographically and politically based units that took little or no account of ethnic distribution. Making matters worse, colonial policy often aimed at discouraging unified native resistance by emphasizing differences between ethnic groups, even pitting them against each other. This proved a major contributing factor in the civil wars that devastated large swaths of the continent in the later part of the 20th century and into the early 21st century, including Nigeria's Biafran War (1967–70) and the Rwanda genocide of 1994.

While colonial powers were dedicated to exploiting their colonies for raw materials, they put little effort into developing their economies. As a result, Africa consists largely of less developed countries (LDCs). When the African states were becoming independent, many looked to the Soviet Union as a model for economic and political development. They embraced socialism, the centrally planned economy, as the path to development. Most of the countries also became one-party dictatorships.

After the collapse of the Soviet Union, African states lost a major source of support. Socialism was quickly discredited as African leaders began to look to the United States and western Europe for help and direction. Market mechanisms were introduced, or at least talked about, as sub-Saharan Africa tried to restart failed economies.

In the 1990s dictators suddenly felt internal pressure to democratize their governments. The record of democratization was uneven. The best news came from South Africa, with the end of apartheid and the first free, all-race multiparty elections in the country's history. Elsewhere, Benin's socialist government collapsed, and the dictator of Mali was overthrown. Kenneth Kaunda of Zambia was defeated in 1991, and in 1994 the longtime dictator of Malawi, Hastings Banda, lost his office in a free election. Rwanda erupted into civil war in 1994. In Zaire (now the Democratic Republic of the Congo) the dictator Mobutu Sese Seko was overthrown in 1997, but rebels continued fighting the government into the 21st century. Other countries that faced civil wars include Angola, the Republic of the Congo, Liberia,

Sierra Leone, and Côte d'Ivoire. Even though most African states broke free of colonialism decades ago, they are still dealing, to different degrees and in different ways, with its long-lasting toxic effects.

amalgamation Combining groups, companies, or bodies into a single entity.

authoritarianism A system or philosophy of government based on the principle that the leader and not the people have the final authority.

capital A stock of resources that may be employed in the production of goods and services. In classical economics it is one of the three factors of production, the others being labour and land.

Commonwealth A free association of sovereign states comprising the United Kingdom and a number of its former dependencies that have chosen to maintain ties of friendship and practical cooperation and that acknowledge the British monarch as symbolic head of their association.

decolonization The process by which colonies become independent of the colonizing country.

franchise A legal right or privilege; in particular, the right to vote.

genocide The deliberate and systematic destruction of a group of people because of their ethnicity, nationality, religion, or race.

gradualist Referring to the policy or strategy of approaching a desired end by gradual stages.

guerrilla Relating to an irregular military force fighting small-scale, limited actions, in concert with an overall political-military strategy, against conventional military forces.

hinterland A region remote from urban areas or cultural centers.

inalienable Not capable of being taken away, given up, or transferred.

jihadist Relating to Muslim groups that wage a holy war on behalf of Islam as a religious duty.

League of Nations An international organization set up to maintain world peace. Established at the end of World War I, it was replaced by the United Nations in 1946.

Mahdist Relating to followers of al-Mahdī (Muḥammad Aḥmad ibn al-Sayyid ʿAbd Allāh), creator of a vast Islamic state extending from the Red Sea to Central Africa, who proclaimed his divine mission was to purify Islam and the governments that defiled it.

mandate A commission granted by the League of Nations to a member nation to administer a territory on its behalf.

mercantilism An economic theory and practice that promoted governmental regulation of a nation's economy for the purpose of augmenting state power. It held that colonies exist for the economic benefit of the mother country and are useless unless they help to achieve profit.

nationalism An ideology based on the premise that a person's loyalty and devotion to the nation-state surpass other individual or group interests. Nationalism as a movement dates to the late 18th century.

negritude A literary movement of the 1930s, '40s, and '50s that began among French-speaking African and Caribbean writers living in Paris as a protest against French colonial rule and the policy of assimilation.

plebiscite A vote by which the people of an entire country or district express an opinion for or against a proposal especially on a choice of government or ruler.

proletariat The lowest social or economic class of a community.

protectorate A relationship between two states, one of which exercises some decisive control over the other.

rhetoric The art of speaking or writing effectively. Also the tone in which information is relayed or arguments are made.

rinderpest An acute, highly contagious viral disease of ruminant animals, primarily cattle, that was once common in Africa, the Indian subcontinent, and the Middle East.

self-determination The process by which a group of people, usually possessing a certain degree of national consciousness, form their own state and choose their own government.

subsistence agriculture Farming that permits people to raise enough food for their own use, with little or none left over for trade.

tariff Also called customs duty, the tax levied upon goods as they cross national boundaries, usually by the government of the importing country. The words "tariff," "duty," and "customs" can be used interchangeably.

viceroy One who rules a country or province as the representative of his sovereign or king and who is empowered to act in the sovereign's name.

BIBLIOGRAPHY

GENERAL

Historical overviews are presented by J.D. Fage and Roland Oliver (eds.), *The Cambridge History of Africa*, 8 vol. (1975–86). UNESCO International Scientific Committee for the Drafting of a General History of Africa, *General History of Africa*, 8 vol. (1981–93), is an international collaborative effort that locates African people and their experience at the centre and portrays African contact with Middle Eastern, Asian, and Euro-American peoples in the larger context of African history. Ali A. Mazrui, *The Africans: A Triple Heritage* (1986), discusses themes that relate to all of Africa.

The psychological impact of colonialism is explored from an African perspective in Frantz Fanon, *The Damned* (1963; also published as *The Wretched of the Earth*, 1963, reissued 1991; originally published in French, 1961). The case against the continuation of Western domination in the period of decolonization is found in Kwame Nkrumah, *Neo-Colonialism: The Last Stage of Imperialism* (1965, reissued 1973).

NORTHERN AFRICA

General works include Elbaki Hermassi, *Leadership and National Development in North Africa: A*

Comparative Study (1972) and Abdallah Laroui (ʿabd Allāh ʿArawi), *The History of the Maghrib: An Interpretive Essay* (1977; originally published in French, 1970). Lucette Valensi, *On the Eve of Colonialism: North Africa Before the French Conquest* (1977; originally published in French, 1969), offers solid interpretation that dispels old myths. Magali Morsy, *North Africa, 1800–1900: A Survey from the Nile Valley to the Atlantic* (1984), is innovative in treating all of northern Africa as a single region. Jacques Berque, *French North Africa: The Maghrib Between Two World Wars* (1967; originally published in French, 1962), is a stimulating but impressionistic account by a leading French scholar. David C. Gordon, *North Africa's French Legacy, 1954–1962* (1962), provides an excellent monograph on the cultural effects of French influence in the region. L. Carl Brown (ed.), *State and Society in Independent North Africa* (1966), provides general interpretive articles on political, economic, and social issues. More recent political developments are covered by David E. Long and Bernard Reich (eds.), *The Government and Politics of the Middle East and North Africa*, 2nd ed. rev. and updated (1986); and Richard B. Parker, *North Africa: Regional Tensions and Strategic Concerns*, rev. and updated ed. (1987).

WESTERN AFRICA

Much original work is available in articles in such journals as *The Journal of African History* (3/yr.); *The International Journal of African Historical Studies* (3/yr.); *History in Africa* (annual); *African Affairs* (quarterly); and *The Journal of Modern African Studies* (quarterly). The standard work is J.F. Ade Ajayi and Michael Crowder (eds.), *History of West Africa*, 2nd ed., 2 vol. (1976–87).

Emmanuel Kwaku Akyeampong, *Themes in West Africa's History* (2006), is a valuable collection of essays exploring various topics in the region's history. Useful atlases include J.D. Fage, *An Atlas of African History*, 2nd ed. (1978); and J.F. Ade Ajayi and Michael Crowder (eds.), *Historical Atlas of Africa* (1985). A short handbook is J.D. Fage, *A History of West Africa*, 4th ed. (1969, reprinted 1992); while Anthony Atmore and Gillian Stacey, *Black Kingdoms, Black Peoples* (1979, reprinted 1985), is a well-illustrated introduction to West African history, peoples, and cultures. Eugene L. Mendonsa, *West Africa: An Introduction to Its History, Civilization and Contemporary Situation* (2002), presents a well-informed overview of the region and its people.

For French-speaking territories, Jean Suret-Canale, *French Colonialism in Tropical Africa, 1900–1945* (1971; originally published in French, 1964), contains useful material; and John D. Hargreaves, *West Africa: The Former French States* (1967), is an excellent short study. Ronald H. Chilcote, *Portuguese Africa* (1967), is a useful general work. Useful works for the prejihad history of western and central Sudan are Nehemia Levtzion, *Ancient Ghana and Mali* (1973, reprinted 1980); the classic work by Edward William Bovill, *The Golden Trade of the Moors*, 2nd ed. rev. by Robin Hallett (1995); J.F.P. Hopkins and Nehemia Levtzion (eds.), *Corpus of Early Arabic Sources for West African History*, 2nd ed. (1981, reprinted 2000); and Pierre-Damien Mvuyekure (ed.), *West African Kingdoms, 500–1590* (2004). P.F. de Moraes Farias, *Arabic Medieval Inscriptions from the Republic of Mali: Epigraphy, Chronicles and Songhay-Tuāreg History* (2003), uses Arabic inscriptions from the 11th–15th century to provide detail on the history of the Songhai and Tuareg.

Three works on the early history of Guinea may be recommended: J.D. Fage, "Upper and Lower Guinea," chapter 6 in *The Cambridge History of Africa*, vol. 3 (1977, reprinted 2001), pp. 463–518; Frank Willett, *Ife in the History of West African*

Sculpture (1967); and Robert Smith, *Kingdoms of the Yoruba*, 3rd ed. (1988). The arrival of the European traders to the Guinea Coast is treated in John W. Blake, *West Africa: Quest for God and Gold, 1454–1578*, 2nd ed. rev. and enlarged (1977). Philip D. Curtin, *The Atlantic Slave Trade: A Census* (1969, reprinted 2010), provides an innovative analysis; but the basic data have been reworked in a useful general history, Paul E. Lovejoy, *Transformations in Slavery*, 3rd ed. (2012).

The subsequent history of Guinea has occasioned many important monographs, such as John Vogt, *Portuguese Rule on the Gold Coast, 1469–1682* (1979); Walter Rodney, *A History of the Upper Guinea Coast, 1545–1800* (1970, reprinted 2006); A.F.C. Ryder, *Benin and the Europeans, 1485–1897* (1969); Ray A. Kea, *Settlements, Trade, and Polities in the Seventeenth-Century Gold Coast* (1982); Philip D. Curtin, *Economic Change in Precolonial Africa* (1975); David Northrup, *Trade Without Rulers: Pre-colonial Economic Development in South-eastern Nigeria* (1978); and Robin Law, *The Oyo Empire, c. 1600–c. 1836* (1977). Robin Law (ed.), *From Slave Trade to Legitimate Commerce: The Commercial Transition in Nineteenth-Century West Africa* (2002), presents an impressive collection of papers that evaluate the region's transition from the exporting of slaves to other, mostly agricultural products. J. Cameron Monroe and Akinwumi Ogundiran (eds.), *Power and Landscape in Atlantic West Africa: Archaeological Perspectives* (2012), explores the sociopolitical development in West Africa during the 17th–19th century through an archaeological lens. Peter B. Clarke, *West Africa and Islam* (1982), covering the 8th to the 20th century; and Ira M. Lapidus, *A History of Islamic Societies*, 3rd ed. (2014), are useful introductory works. The great outburst of Islam in western Africa in the 18th and 19th centuries is covered in Murray Last, *The Sokoto Caliphate* (1967, reprinted 1977); and David Robinson, *The Holy War of Umar Tal: The Western Sudan in the Mid-nineteenth Century* (1985).

The growth of European influence is covered in works such as Robin Hallet, *The Penetration of Africa: European Enterprise and Exploration Principally in Northern and Western Africa up to 1815* (1965); A. Adu Boahen, *Britain, the Sahara, and the Western Sudan, 1788–1861* (1964, reprinted 1970); Philip D. Curtin, *The Image of Africa: British Ideas and Action, 1780–1850* (1964, reissued 1973); Kenneth Onwuka Dike, *Trade and Politics in the Niger Delta, 1830–1885* (1956, reprinted 2008); and J.F. Ade Ajayi, *Christian Missions in Nigeria,*

1841–1891 (1965, reprinted 1981). For the European partition of western Africa, the standard works are John D. Hargreaves, *Prelude to the Partition of West Africa* (1963, reprinted 1970), and *West Africa Partitioned*, 2 vol. (1974–85); but also important are Henri Brunschwig, *French Colonialism, 1871–1914: Myths and Realities* (1966; originally published in French, 1960); and A.S. Kanya-Forstner, *The Conquest of the Western Sudan: A Study in French Military Imperialism* (1969, reprinted 2009).

For the colonial period, two contemporary studies are invaluable: Lord Hailey (William Malcolm Hailey), *An African Survey*, rev. ed. (1957, reprinted 1968); and S. Herbert Frankel, *Capital Investment in Africa: Its Course and Effects* (1938, reprinted 1969). For indirect rule, Margery Perham, *Native Administration in Nigeria* (1937, reprinted 1989), is a classic. A general synthesis is provided by Michael Crowder, *West Africa Under Colonial Rule* (1968, reprinted 1981). Also of note are Michael Crowder and Obaro Ikime (eds.), *West African Chiefs: Their Changing Status Under Colonial Rule and Independence* (1970); Sean Hanretta, *Islam and Social Change in French West Africa* (2009); Michael Crowder (ed.), *West African Resistance: The Military Response to Colonial Occupation*, new ed. (1978); and F. Ugboaja Ohaegbulam, *West African*

Responses to European Imperialism in the Nineteenth and Twentieth Centuries (2002). The chapters on western Africa in L.H. Gann and Peter Duignan (eds.), *Colonialism in Africa, 1870–1960*, 2 vol. (1969–70, reprinted 1988), can be extremely valuable. There is much useful material in two collections: Prosser Gifford and Wm. Roger Louis (eds.), *Britain and Germany in Africa: Imperial Rivalry and Colonial Rule* (1967, reprinted 2004), and *France and Britain in Africa: Imperial Rivalry and Colonial Rule* (1971, reprinted 1978). Martin A. Klein, *Slavery and Colonial Rule in French West Africa* (1998), focuses on Senegal, Guinea, and Mali.

Works dealing with the transition to independence include John D. Hargreaves, *The End of Colonial Rule in West Africa* (1979), and *Decolonization in Africa*, 2nd ed. (1996, reprinted in 2014); Toyin Falola (ed.), *The End of Colonial Rule: Nationalism and Decolonization* (2002); Ken Post, *The New States of West Africa*, rev. ed. (1968); Ruth Schachter Morgenthau, *Political Parties in French-Speaking West Africa* (1964, reprinted 1970); Prosser Gifford and Wm. Roger Louis (eds.), *The Transfer of Power in Africa: Decolonization, 1940–1960* (1982); Edward Mortimer, *France and the Africans, 1944–1960* (1969); and Tony Chafer, *The End of Empire in*

French West Africa: France's Successful Decolonization? (2002).

CENTRAL AFRICA

Joseph C. Miller, *Kings and Kinsmen* (1976), is an innovative study of the use of oral evidence for the construction of Central African history; his *Way of Death: Merchant Capitalism and the Angolan Slave Trade, 1730–1830* (1988) is mainly concerned with south-central Africa but illustrates the history of the slave trade in ways not hitherto attempted. Robert W. Harms, *River of Wealth, River of Sorrow: The Central Zaire Basin in the Era of the Slave and Ivory Trade, 1500–1891* (1981), is one of the great classics of Central African history. Thomas Q. Reefe, *The Rainbow and the Kings: A History of the Luba Empire to 1891* (1981), significantly revises previous interpretations of the leading inland empire of Central Africa. Charles Perrings, *Black Mineworkers in Central Africa* (1979), offers a radical history of the Katanga copper mines. Eugenia W. Herbert, *Red Gold of Africa: Copper in Precolonial History and Culture* (1984), is a brilliantly innovative and deeply researched cultural history. René Lemarchand, *Rwanda and Burundi* (1970), discusses the early history of these countries.

Sidney Langford Hinde, *The Fall of the Congo Arabs* (1897, reprinted 1969), offers an eyewitness account of the colonial conquest of eastern Congo (Kinshasa) in the 1890s. Adam Hochschild, *King Leopold's Ghost: A Story of Greed, Terror, and Heroism in Colonial Africa* (1998), discusses the exploitation of African labour in what became the Belgian Congo. William Roger Louis, *Ruanda-Urundi, 1884–1919* (1963, reprinted 1979), provides a diplomatic history of the German enclave in Central Africa. Thomas Pakenham, *The Scramble for Africa: White Man's Conquest of the Dark Continent from 1876 to 1912* (1991), examines European expansion on the continent of Africa. Patrick Manning, *Francophone Sub-Saharan Africa, 1880–1985* (1988), discusses the colonization and then decolonization of parts of Central Africa. David Birmingham and Phyllis M. Martin (eds.), *History of Central Africa: The Contemporary Years Since 1960* (1998), examines countries in the region to elucidate their postcolonial experience. Tamara Giles-Vernick, *Cutting the Vines of the Past: Environmental Histories of the Central African Rain Forest* (2002), focuses on the differing views that Africans and Europeans have of Africa's environment. Marie-Louise Martin, *Kimbangu: An African Prophet and His Church* (1975; originally published in German, 1971), studies the independent church of Congo (Kinshasa). Of the many books on the genocide in Rwanda and Burundi, two of the best are Gérard Prunier, *The Rwanda Crisis: History of a Genocide*, expanded (1998); and René Lemarchand, *Burundi: Ethnic Conflict and Genocide* (1996).

EASTERN AFRICA

Bethwell A. Ogot (ed.), *Zamani: A Survey of East African History*, new ed. (1974), is still the best single-volume survey. Roland A. Oliver et al. (eds.), *History of East Africa*, 3 vol. (1963–76), constitutes the most ambitious account so far. P.L. Shinnie (ed.), *The African Iron Age* (1971), contains authoritative articles on archaeology by H.N. Chittick, "The Coast of East Africa," ch. 5, and by J.E.G. Sutton, "The Interior of East Africa," ch. 6. *Azania* (annual), issued by the British Institute in Eastern Africa, includes authoritative "precolonial" articles. G.S.P. Freeman-Grenville, *The Medieval History of the Coast of Tanganyika* (1962), although subject now to correction, is still valuable. C.S. Nicholls, *The Swahili Coast: Politics, Diplomacy, and Trade on the East African Littoral, 1798–1856* (1971), is a very full study. Frederick Cooper, *Plantation Slavery on the East Coast of*

Africa (1977), provides an excellent socioeconomic study of Zanzibar and Kenya in the 19th century. R.M.A. Van Zwanenberg and Anne King, *An Economic History of Kenya and Uganda, 1800–1970* (1975), concentrates on the years after 1900.

The only book to deal with the history of the Horn of Africa is John Markakis, *National and Class Conflict in the Horn of Africa* (1987). Since there is no established historiography, the history of the entire Horn must be constructed from such works devoted to Somalia and Ethiopia as Harold G. Marcus, *A History of Ethiopia* (1994), the only modern general history of Ethiopia from *Australopithecus afarensis* to the fall of the Derg in 1991; and I.M. Lewis, *A Modern History of Somalia: Nation and State in the Horn of Africa*, rev., updated, and expanded ed. (1988), a comprehensive treatment of the political history of affairs in all the Somali territories. I.M. Lewis (ed.), *Nationalism & Self Determination in the Horn of Africa* (1983), discusses the rival ethnic nationalisms of the Horn, including those at the centre and periphery of Ethiopia. Works on the history of the Somali-Ethiopian conflict include Tom J. Farer, *War Clouds on the Horn of Africa: The Widening Storm*, 2nd rev. ed. (1979); and Robert F. Gorman, *Political Conflict on the*

Horn of Africa (1981), which highlights the Ogaden war of 1977–78.

SOUTHERN AFRICA

Neil Parsons, *A New History of Southern Africa*, 2nd ed. (1993), is an introductory text dealing with the region as a whole. David Birmingham and Phyllis Martin (eds.), *History of Central Africa*, 2 vol. (1983), contains essays on topics in Central and Southern African history. A.J. Wills, *An Introduction to the History of Central Africa: Zambia, Malawi, and Zimbabwe*, 4th ed. (1985), is still a useful guide to British south-central Africa. John Iliffe, *The African Poor: A History* (1987), discusses poverty throughout Africa's history. Leroy Vail and Landeg White, *Power and the Praise Poem: Southern African Voices in History* (1991), signals a major turning point in the interpretation of Southern Africa's past by insisting on the centrality of African interpretations through poetry, performance, and other oral expressions. John Reader, *Africa: A Biography of the Continent* (1997), is a good introduction to themes relating to Africa. Current research can be found in such specialist journals as *Journal of African History* (3/yr.); *Journal of*

Southern African Studies (quarterly); and *African Affairs* (quarterly).

Portuguese ventures in west-central and east-central Africa are chronicled in Edward A. Alpers, *Ivory and Slaves* (also published as *Ivory & Slaves in East Central Africa*, 1975); and Jan Vansina, *Kingdoms of the Savanna* (1966). Slavery in the region is discussed in Joseph C. Miller, *Way of Death: Merchant Capitalism and the Angolan Slave Trade, 1730–1830* (1988); and John Thornton, *Africa and Africans in the Making of the Atlantic World, 1400–1800*, 2nd ed. (1998).

Donald Denoon and Balam Nyeko, *Southern Africa Since 1800*, new ed. (1984), is a good overview. A stimulating account of the colonial period can be found in Martin Chanock, *Law, Custom, and Social Order: The Colonial Experience in Malawi and Zambia* (1985). Attempts to look at the African side in this period include Robert Ross, *Adam Kok's Griquas: A Study in the Development of Stratification in South Africa* (1976); Norman Etherington, *Preachers, Peasants, and Politics in Southeast Africa, 1835–80: African Christian Communities in Natal, Pondoland, and Zululand* (1978); and Donald Crummey (ed.), *Banditry, Rebellion and Social Protest in Africa* (1986). The era of mineral discoveries and the scramble for Southern Africa are the subject of Geoffrey Wheatcroft, *The Randlords* (1986); and Randall M. Packard, *White Plague, Black Labor: Tuberculosis and the Political Economy of Health and Disease in South Africa* (1989). The scramble for Africa and the establishment of colonial society are dealt with in Thomas Pakenham, *The Scramble for Africa: White Man's Conquest of the Dark Continent from 1876 to 1912* (1991); and Bill Freund, *The Making of Contemporary Africa: The Development of African Society Since 1800*, 2nd ed. (1998). Events in Angola and Mozambique are outlined in Malyn Newitt, *Portugal in Africa: The Last Hundred Years* (1981), a lucid overview with a synopsis of the earlier period of Portuguese rule; and Gervase Clarence-Smith, *The Third Portuguese Empire, 1825–1975: A Study in Economic Imperialism* (1985), an overview from an economic perspective.

Martin Chanock, *Britain, Rhodesia, and South Africa, 1900–45* (also published as *Unconsummated Union*, 1977), contains a masterly account of interregional politics. Coverage of more recent events from differing viewpoints can be found in Basil Davidson, Joe Slovo, and Anthony R. Wilkinson, *Southern Africa: The New Politics of Revolution* (1976), on the struggle in the Portuguese colonies, South Africa, and Rhodesia following the Portuguese coup of 1974. Margaret Jean Hay and Sharon Stichter (eds.), *African Women South of the Sahara*, 2nd ed. (1995), discusses women and their roles in African society. Prosser Gifford and W. Roger Louis (eds.), *Decolonization and African Independence: The Transfers of Power, 1960–1980* (1988), considers the decolonization process.